Across Three Oceans

To ALAN.

with lots of
love from scruff.

X .

Across Three Oceans

CONOR O'BRIEN

GRANADA
London Toronto Sydney New York

Granada Publishing Limited
8 Grafton Street, London W1X 3LA

First published 1927
This edition published by Granada Publishing 1984
Reprinted 1985

British Library Cataloguing in Publication Data

O'Brien, Conor
   Across three oceans.
   1. Saoirse (*Ship*)   2. Voyages around the
   world
   I. Title
   910.4'1   G440

ISBN 0-246-12309-5

Printed in Great Britain by
Billing & Sons Ltd., Worcester

CONTENTS

MAPS AND DIAGRAMS

INTRODUCTION

IT seems almost presumptuous for one whose longest continuous sea passages have not much exceeded a thousand miles to express an opinion upon a great voyage consisting of many passages each several thousand miles in length. But experience of small things may enable one to appreciate great achievements, even though one can never hope to emulate them.

On June 20, 1923, the yacht *Saoirse*, of 20 tons Thames measurement, left Dublin bound for the Cape. Besides the owner, Mr. Conor O Brien, the crew consisted of two hands. They had fair winds as far as Cape Verde Islands. In about lat. 4° S., long. 24° W., soon after picking up the south-east Trades the mast-head was found to be badly sprung, necessitating a visit to Pernambuco for repairs. As the yacht was not copper-sheathed a scrub also had become an imperative necessity. Leaving Pernambuco on September 1, *Saoirse* made a good passage to the Cape in thirty-five days, the average day's run being 111 miles, thus completing the first stage of the voyage round the world.

With a new crew Mr. O Brien left Port Natal on December 11, bound for Melbourne. A Mercator course was steered, and though *Saoirse* made her easting in no higher latitude than about 38° she found plenty of wind. This passage of about 5,700 miles was made in fifty-one days. A passage from Melbourne to Auckland, New Zealand, completed the second stage of the voyage.

Saoirse left Auckland on October 22, 1924, bound homeward round Cape Horn, having as crew, besides the owner, a Polynesian and two other seamen. After the first ten or twelve days, to the southward of the fortieth parallel in "the roaring forties" they got the true Westerlies which carried them across the South Pacific, round the Horn, and well up towards the Falklands. On December 6, *Saoirse* arrived in Stanley Harbour, Falklands, forty-six days out from Auckland, distance 5,800 miles. Mr. O Brien's plain seamanlike account is so modestly written that a casual reader might miss its full significance. But anyone who knows anything of the sea, following the course of the vessel day by day on the chart, will realize the good seamanship, vigilance and endurance required to drive this little bluff-bowed vessel, with her foul uncoppered bottom, at speeds of from 150 to 170 miles a day, as well as the weight of wind and sea which must sometimes have been encountered.

Saoirse left the Falkland Islands on February 28, 1925, and making a short stay at Pernambuco and at the island of Fayal, Azores, arrived in Dublin on June 20.

For the three stages of this voyage round the world Mr. O Brien was awarded the Challenge Cup of the Royal Cruising Club three times in succession. To show what a very high standard of seamanship and enterprise this implies, it may be recalled that three years earlier a fine cruise in a small yacht from England to the West Indies just failed to win the Cup. During the past thirty-five years small yacht cruising has developed so rapidly that the great adventure of one decade becomes the commonplace of the next. But however common long voyages in small yachts may become, Mr. O Brien will always be remembered for his voyage across the South Pacific and round the Horn.

Saoirse's great voyage inevitably recalls the late

INTRODUCTION

Lieutenant Muhlhauser's circumnavigation of the globe in *Amaryllis*. But there can be no rivalry, for the routes were entirely different, the former relying mainly upon the Westerlies and the latter upon the Trades, and, rigged as they were, neither vessel could very well have accomplished what the other did.

CLAUD WORTH.

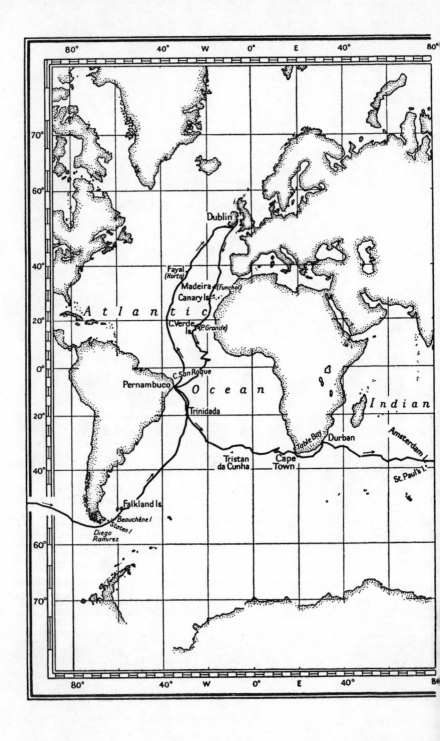

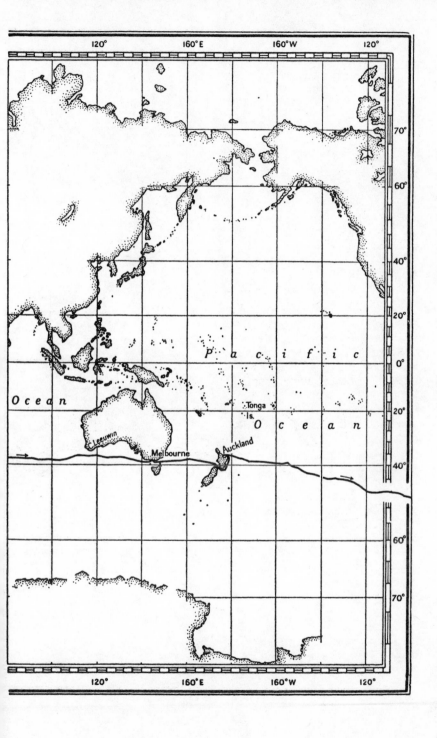

CHAPTER I

WAYS AND MEANS

THERE are, according to the tetrahedral view of the earth, four oceans; but of these three only are generally necessary to navigation, for the Arctic Ocean is only used by Polar bears and Polar explorers, and in any case is not navigable. How I came to cross the remaining three is quickly told. I was invited to join a mountaineering party in the New Zealand Alps at Christmas, 1923, and having a nearly new yacht I regarded this as an excellent opportunity of finding out the merits or demerits of her design, which was of my own making.

There are two ways of getting to and from New Zealand. One can go from East to West, running down one's longitude in the very constant Trade Winds, but considerably hampered by land; or from West to East in the Roaring Forties, where indeed the winds are not so trustworthy, but the sea is clear of obstructions. The calms in the Gulf of Panama closed the former route to me who have no auxiliary power. To digress for a moment, the foolish question which is most often asked of me is "How did you manage without a motor?" By following that track on which a sailing vessel goes the faster. I ran down my easting, sometimes to my great discomfort in the thirties, more happily in the forties, and for twelve days without incident, though with some trepidation, in the fifties. I struck a mean between the safe but devious track of John Company's frigates, too slow for my supplies of stores and water, and the ice-strewn path of the huge emigrant clippers, too stormy for my little boat of twenty tons.

Let it not be supposed, however, that my route was chosen purely from utilitarian motives. In 1923 the cult of the sailing ship, a purely archæological interest, be it understood, was flourishing; and like many another devotee I was scouring second-hand bookshops in seaport towns for logs of the Colonial passage. There was a good deal of sentiment in the impulse that sent me forth, as far as my circumstances permitted, in the wake of the *Lightning* or the *Oweenee*; together with a certain amount of curiosity as to what a really big sea looked like; a curiosity which, I imagine, I had already satisfied as far as one can satisfy these things and live, off the West Coast of Ireland. And at the back of everything I had a feeling that I, a first-voyager, ought to be initiated into the mysteries of the ocean on one of the classic passages; which, once accomplished, would give me the right to experiment with a small fore-and-after on the wind and current charts of the world at large.

Here follows, then, my version of a voyage round the world in a sailing vessel, a version which is, in view of the small size of the vessel, unreasonable neither in track nor in time; marred by only one serious lapse from orthodoxy, which was my misfortune rather than my fault. Your South-Seaman commonly sighted Madeira and the Cape Verde Islands; I called at both, because I was a yachtsman. He often got foul of the Brazilian Coast; even the *James Baines* on her first voyage of sixty-three days to Melbourne got to leeward of Cape San Roque; I made the land on the right side of that Cape, and only to get repairs for a sprung mast-head. Sailing from Pernambuco I cleared the rest of South America without making a tack, and had a tolerably good run to Table Bay, observing that in the South Atlantic the winds were out of all order and reason. It was after Table Bay that the lapse from orthodoxy occurred, and the tragedy that sent me into Durban, a place which is most accursed in the matter of winds and should not be on the itinerary of any sailing vessel; but from which after a fortnight of baffling winds I reached the westerlies of the Indian Ocean. It would have been pedantic to have passed by Melbourne, when that port lay only 50 miles away; besides, we were almost out of potatoes.

Here I will anticipate the second most frequent question, "How did you do about stores and water?" by saying that we did very well. On this occasion, fifty days out from our last port, we gave the Melbourne pilot a five-course dinner which was highly commended. We did not ask him to drink water, for we had still some delicious Cape wine left. But if he had been of that persuasion we could have offered him water, and good water at that. One of the great blessings of modern civilization is that one can get good water almost anywhere; and another is that one has galvanized tanks to carry it in. At least, in spite of warnings to the contrary from the health faddists, I took all my water as it was given me without question, and did not chlorinate it or filter it or boil it, or in any other way spoil its flavour or its freshness or, I suppose, its bacterial content; and I never opened up the main tank since it was put aboard in 1922. Generally speaking, one can, I think, take far more liberties in this respect in tropical countries than one can at home; in the larger ports, the kind of ports where there are any facilities at all for taking in water, the supply simply has to be good or the natives would die of it. For the same reason the streets simply have to be kept clean; and, in consequence, despite a very mixed population, few of whom have ever attended lectures on hygiene, such cities as Pernambuco and Durban are conspicuously healthy.

We reckoned to carry three months' supply of necessities and two months' of ordinary good living. It was because we lived extravagantly well that we had to make fifty-day passages our maximum. At one time, to give my crew an interest in setting sail, I threatened them with an allowance of salt beef and hard tack; but they, arguing quite justly that the little they could do would not help the ship along much and that I, for my own sake, would see to the passage-making, did not respond to the stimulus. It was supposed that with everything which would hold water full we carried 200 gallons. The tanks were connected to a very handy pump in the pantry, and as this had no lock on it, no record of consumption was kept. We never suspected ourselves of running short, however, and three or four days before reaching port we used fresh water for washing—needless to say at other times we had to wait for a shower of rain.

After Melbourne I went to New Zealand, too late of course for the mountaineering; too late, as it turned out, even to start home at once; so, having spent some time putting men into and taking them out of various hospitals along the coast, I finished the outward voyage at Auckland.

The homeward passage was entirely orthodox. I steered the approved course from East Cape to Diego Ramirez; I put in, most properly, to the Falkland Islands, being again short of potatoes. Potatoes are the seaman's greatest curse; there are only three places in the world where they are worth taking on board: Ireland, Argentina, and Tristan da Cunha. I made a tolerable passage up the South Atlantic, but had to put in to Pernambuco (which after all is hardly out of the way; and it would have been churlish not to have revisited my friends there) to land a sick man. In the North-East Trade I held so good a wind that I did not have to go at all out of my way to land two sick men at Fayal in the Western Islands; and so home.

Thus did I steer according to the recommendations of the textbooks; other yachtsmen may ask whether I recommend this track to them. On the whole, yes; as far as my experience goes. But of the Southern Ocean and its habits I know practically nothing; it put on its best behaviour for my benefit, and the most consistently bad weather I met was in lat. 32° S.! Nor did I meet inconveniently fresh Trade Winds, and I confess that before I started I was more afraid of the 1,250 miles from the Equator to Trinidada than of four times that distance across the South Pacific. But I think I should die of boredom if I had to run 5,000 miles in the Trades. The runs on the Southern passage are not necessarily long; that from New Zealand to the Falkland Islands or Punta Arenas alone exceeds 5,000 miles; but unfortunately, unless one has a taste for Antarctic icebergs, they do not lead the traveller into strange or interesting places. No one wants to go to Fernando do Noronha; the landing on Trinidada is generally impossible; it is more than likely that by now the rats have eaten all the potatoes on Tristan da Cunha. And as for the other places, Baedeker and Murray have said all there is to say about them.

I confess to a regret that I did not visit Port Harberton, the most southerly place in the world that is permanently inhabited; but one wants fine weather to explore the sounds at the back of Cape Horn, and I preferred to use my fine weather to get away out of that neighbourhood. In fact the only generally unknown region that I visited was that about Graham Land on the Antarctic Continent, and that I did not in my own vessel but in the mail steamer; however, as this is the only part of my travelling of any general interest I allow some account of it into these pages. For the rest my travelling was a strictly sea-going affair, and my account of it is written primarily for those who dream of long ocean passages in a small yacht, and more particularly for those who have sufficient technical equipment, both material and mental, to hope that some day their dreams will come true. And I hope it may be read by some of those who by their records of passages in big ships in the course of trade have made possible the passage of a small ship on pleasure, and that it may remind them of the days when they walked fore-and-aft on the poop instead of thwartships on the bridge, with their eyes on the royal leach instead of on the standard compass.

This was my way of sailing round the world; a way every mile of which can be enjoyed by those who still pin their faith to sail, probably the only way on which an engine would be no manner of use. When I am making short runs along the coast I am annoyed because I feel my sailing boat is not efficient. Ten years ago she would go where I wanted her to, but now (to follow the herd) I want her to go where she will not. To enjoy her qualities one wants to see her blow across an ocean at the rate of a thousand miles a week; then one knows she is the most efficient thing that ever floated. My ideal sailing boat, be it understood; the means I employed to sail round the world were not ideal. My poor *Saoirse* was taken from the West of Ireland, for which waters she was designed, and sent forth to be driven round the Southern Ocean, for which trade she was disproportionately short. Yet I do not like to dogmatize about shipbuilding, a business in which theory often lets one down badly. Solomon, I think it was, said that one of the things no fellow could understand was the way of a ship in the sea; and I cannot understand how my ship has an economical speed of 7 knots with a waterline length of 37½ feet.

With the aid of a few other dimensions and the drawings on pp. 24 and 27 I will try to describe this vessel, which was built for me at Baltimore in County Cork. She is 42 feet long over all, with a beam of 12 feet and a normal draft of about 6¾. The general type of hull was suggested by a fishing-boat built at Arklow some time, I imagine, in the 'sixties; a decided throw-back for a yacht launched in 1922; but I had been to sea in that fishing-boat and knew her good qualities. She had that very doubtful blessing, a ketch rig, and a bad ketch rig at that, for the vessel being so short of mainmast is stepped too far forward in order to get a big mainsail and a big saloon; and this makes her trim by the head when running. One has, however, to sacrifice most things to accommodation in a cruising yacht, especially if one has to live on board for two years continously in all latitudes. I do not say in all climates, for I did not go to the places where one suffers extremes of heat, cold, or wet. The cabin being then the principal considera-

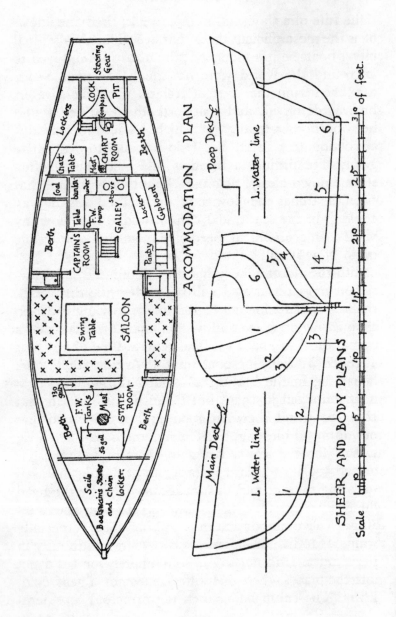

ACCOMMODATION PLAN

SHEER AND BODY PLANS

Scale [0 5 10 15 20 25 30 of feet.]

Main Deck

L. Water line

Poop Deck

L. water line

SALOON

STATE ROOM.

CAPTAIN'S ROOM

CHART ROOM

GALLEY

PIT

COCK

Berth

Berth

Berth

Berth

Lockers

Coal

water

bunker

Chart Table

Captain's Table

F.W. pump

Locker

Cupboard

Pantry

Stove

Mast

Swing Table

F.W. Tanks

Mast

So gall

130 gall

Sails

Boatswain's Stores and chain Locker.

steering gear

compass

tion, I planned it on a generous scale, to the exclusion of any forecastle; a fact which made the subsequent introduction of the foremast hand rather embarrassing. In the result, I have a fair two-berth cabin forward; a noble saloon; abaft this my own room on the starboard side of the companion and the pantry, which I need hardly say is generally flooded when we are on the starboard tack, on the port side. Beyond this is the galley, the pride of the ship; in which is a gigantic stove, the comforter of our stormy hours off the Horn, but a sad coal-eater. In such a galley the veriest tyro could not fail to turn out good meals; and on the homeward voyage I had an excellent, indeed a professional, cook. Now it will be understood why we lived in more comfort and brought ourselves home in better condition than is common on a voyage of this kind, for the majority of small yachts try to cook in their forecastles, the very worst place for such a delicate and important operation.

On deck I have a chart-room; it is technically a deckhouse, for I never inquire whether the man at the wheel is inside or outside of it, or inside or outside of the spare bunk constructed therein. A chartroom is an absolute necessity; if one tries to do one's navigation in the saloon one is certain before long to spread out a chart on the top of the butter-dish. Besides one wants a place to keep one's charts flat, especially if one has over a hundred of them; one wants to keep one's Nautical Almanac out of the shelf where the novels are; one wants a way of laying one's hand on any of the infinite paraphernalia of navigation. And it is very comforting to be able to sit in a snug warm room liberally lit by acetylene (this also serves the saloon, galley, and navigation lights) and steer with one hand only out in the rain.

In the fore-peak chains, sails, ropes, wood, coal, water, oil, and so on, do not quite take up all the space, for my prophetic spirit had made it quite ridiculously big; though it did not prophesy the inordinate size of some people's mail-bags; I have been in places so ill-provided with steam communication that I have carried mails on thousand-mile passages.

In order to get all this into a 20-tonner without indulging in an undue amount of freeboard, for I like good high bulwarks and one cannot have both, I made a poop-deck 10 feet long and a cabin top all the way to the mainmast, both raised 15 inches above the main deck. Not only does the poop-deck give me room for the chart-house bunk, but it gives the helmsman a dry place to sit on; not only does the cabin top give headroom below, but it makes a safe place to stow gear on. Everything would be perfect were it not that the work was done in the middle of the Civil War, when we had to depend on our own very scanty resources; and one wants the best of material and workmanship to make a broken deck like this watertight.

This hull, with its full midship section and fine ends, especially aft, drifts along on an air in smooth water, or will stand up to her canvas well enough to maintain her position in a moderate gale. Considering that all her ballast, of scrap-iron indifferently stowed, is inside, the ship is extraordinarily stiff, and was undoubtedly improved by the heavier mast I got in Cape Town. But excessive stability is easily cured by taking out some ballast; and the extra buoyancy is a great asset when running down the easting. But when one has a long

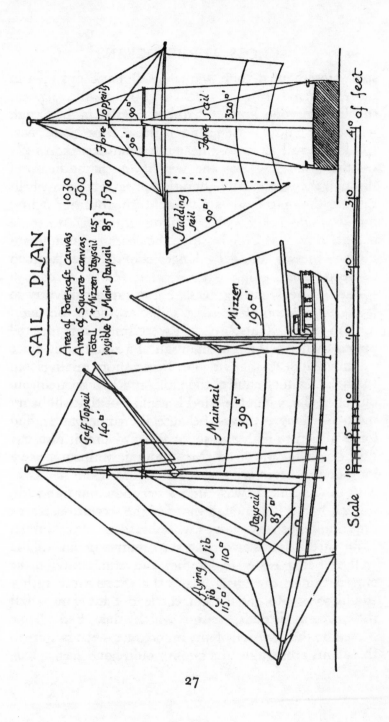

SAIL PLAN

Area of Fore&aft Canvas 1030
Area of Square Canvas   500
Total {+ Mizzen Staysail 45} 1570
possible {+ Main Staysail 85}

Fore Topsail 90ᵈ'
90ᵈ'
Fore Sail 320ᵈ'
Studding Sail 90ᵈ'

Mizzen 190ᵈ'

Gaff Topsail 140ᵈ'
Mainsail 390ᵈ'
Staysail 85ᵈ'
Flying Jib 115ᵈ'
Jib 110ᵈ'

Scale '10

0   5   10   20   30   40 of feet

27

spell close-hauled, one wants it all back again, and more. When I drove my boat at 8 knots in a big sea, she let everyone know all about it; she had not the length to enjoy herself under these conditions. Nor would she sail anywhere near the wind except in light weather; she had not the weight to thrust her way through the waves. Any alteration of rig which involved shifting the mast farther aft would improve her sailing but it would also involve spoiling my cabins to some extent. Now that I am back on the coast I shall tolerate her weaknesses, and get a longer ship if I ever want to go deep-water again.

Bad as her masting was, I did not aggravate its faults by a window-dressing sail plan, as is too common in ketch yachts; my sails were small, but they all pulled their weight. The mainsail of a ketch is always a nuisance at sea, since its foot, being short relatively to the hoist, cannot control the gaff; and it is particularly objectionable when the wind is well aft—as it will be on most of a long passage—because the principal driving force is then so high and so far forward that it puts the ship down by the head. My mainsail was not a very lofty one to begin with, and having no boom it was so easy to reef that it was often a very low one; and the mizzen had a big enough share of the work to preserve the trim. I was very pleased with this boomless mainsail; I am sure it is easier on the ship than a boom sail, as well as being easier to handle, and eliminating those cursed things, the lifts. True, the sheets were rather troublesome—to get the correct lead they came abaft the mizzen shrouds, round which they had to be passed on the occasion of any manœuvre—but in spite of this all my crews agreed a boom would have been worse.

My jib did not accord with British practice. I do not like shifting jibs, a difficult and sometimes dangerous operation; so mine was hanked to a stay. It was set during the whole voyage, except on four days when we were hove-to; and then I fancy it was easier to stow than to take in a jib set flying. It was a smallish sail, so its clew could not foul the forestay, and hang up on or get damaged by it; a point well worth considering.

By the time we reached Australia we had evolved a working disposition of fore-and-aft sails which was very efficient in a wind of the strength that suited it; and fortunately that was the average strength of wind which we met. Most days we could carry a small flying jib, set on the three-foot pole of the jib-boom; with the two usual headsails, reefed mainsail, and mizzen, the total area was a little under 800 square feet; just enough, in the circumstances, for our displacement of 24 tons. No part of the sails was more than 25 feet above the deck, so the rolling of the ship did not affect them seriously.

I think it is most important in rigging a vessel for an ocean passage to keep the heavy sails small and low. But topsails may be large and must be light; it does not matter if they are shapeless and baggy. One rarely meets a good breeze together with a sea smooth enough to justify an extension of flat-setting and therefore heavy canvas. It must be remembered that topsails will often be taken in when they are wet, and stowed away for indefinite periods; so they should be of such a texture that they will dry quickly and not take up too much space in the sail-room.

One is not long at sea before one realizes that the comfort and speed of a passage depend less on fore-and-afters than on square canvas; by which I do not necessarily mean sails of rectangular shape, but those set on yards slung midway of their length forward of the mast; it is the yards rather than the sails that are square. A small and short-handed craft might carry a foresail the shape of an inverted triangle, so that a single tackle could serve the purpose of both tacks and sheets—such a sail as is in fact carried by some modern barques as mainsail and crossjack—but we were more ambitious, and the sail hereinafter called a foresail was approximately a square.

When we started its functions were ill-defined, but limited; it could only be used with the wind well abaft the beam. But no very serious alterations were needed to widen its scope—only the fitting of catheads for the tacks—as the yard could be braced up as sharp as we had any use for. This is seldom practicable in yachts, on account of the lead of the topmast backstays; but mine led down at an angle of 30° abaft the mast, to which the spreaders were hinged so that the lee one was easily dragged inboard by the yard. This feature was planned before I had any idea of square sails, to avoid the need for preventer backstays; it was one of the lucky accidents which contributed so much to the success of the voyage. For I soon found out that a square foresail is not merely a substitute for a spinnaker; except for close-hauled work it is vastly superior to a gaff mainsail. As the sheet is eased it becomes more and more a lifting sail, whereas the mainsail remains always a pressing one. It was with the greatest reluctance that we took the foresail in. But we had to do so whenever the wind came before the beam; the sail interfered with the mainsail, and the lee brace, when hauled taut, chafed it—once so badly that we split the leach of the mainsail through two cloths. That the split did not go any farther was due to the fact that those cloths ran up and down, as they should for serious work; a cross-cut sail would probably have torn right across.

This foresail hauled out to the yard-arms on hoops, which was sound in principle, though the hoops were a mistake, for they jammed against and got broken by the rigging. After I got home I bent it on a track under the yard; and I think that is the right way to deal with it on a boat of such a size that one cannot send a hand aloft to pick it up on the yard. In the end we rigged it so that it could be furled satisfactorily from the deck.

The two raffee topsails which I had made at Capetown worked excellently from the start. Their tacks, to which the downhauls were attached, were hanked to the forestay, and slid up and down it, so it was practically impossible for them to take charge while being lowered. When the gaff-topsail was set the lee one was of course not used as such, but it could be bent to a boat-hook and hoisted upside down as a lower stunsail. As *Saoirse* was then rigged with a very high jib-stay, we had to use two topsails to avoid the excessive roach in the foot of a single one; but experiments with this (after the stay had been lowered) did not show any advantage to set against the increased difficulty of handling it.

I have described a rig which is rather complicated but, in my opinion, none the worse for that, if one has a crew; it is far better for their morale to keep them busy making and trimming sail than to set them to work-up jobs or leave them idle. But what if one is left without a crew? Can one make a boat steer herself? I think this is a question of rig—assuming, of course, that the hull is of the right form for any sort of deep-sea work, with a long straight keel and fairly upright stern-post. She might run under square sails only, but that is not for the single-hander. Captain Waller's ingenious running sails would hardly do for a vessel bigger than his *Imogen*. It is a case for fore-and-afters, under which *Saoirse* ran 436 miles in 3 days with a quarterly wind and almost without attention; mainly, I suggest, by virtue of the two jibs which she carried on an unusually long boom.

Prospective navigators may ask whether *Saoirse's* passages were faster or slower than one might expect of a 20-tonner with an average crew. On the whole, I should say, not slower, and very certainly easier and more comfortable; for if the ship was unsuited to the voyage the weather she met on it was exceptionally favourable. She took 280 sailing days over the whole trip of about 31,000 miles. As more than half of this lay between the parallels of 35° and 55° S., the allowance of gales, four in all, was ridiculously small. And as she passed twice through the Doldrums and both belts of Tropical calms, the days on which she made good less than 50 miles (which I reckoned as calms) ought to have been more than ten; especially as half of them occurred in places where a sailing vessel has no business to be. We averaged 4½ knots on the outward voyage, and 5 on the homeward; across the Pacific we did 5¼. It was done rather by avoiding bad runs than by achieving particularly good ones; we could show nothing like that day's work of 214 miles made by the longer but narrower *Seaweed*, nor her week of 1,242; our best was 1,130 in a week of 166 hours. But then I had not the *Seaweed's* crew.

WAYS AND MEANS

It seems incredible to me that anyone should ship for a voyage like that of *Saoirse* unless he were going to take an interest in the sailing of the ship; but except for the mate who started with me and the one that saw me home no one displayed any enthusiasm and very few even common intelligence in the matter. I can smile at their little peculiarities now; at the man who was supposed to be a certificated officer and could not splice a three-strand rope, and who introduced a friend as being a handy man, and the friend cleaned my best file with emery cloth; at the man who could not go on deck even in the Tropics without putting on rubber thigh-boots; at the man who, when told to grease the chain splice in the gaff-topsail sheet, smeared the whole length of the rope, a very small and hard one, with tallow; at the man who jammed the brake of the windlass, and let go the anchor by lifting the pawl and tried to check the chain by dropping it in again; or at the two who started to turn a reef out of the mainsail by letting go the reef tackle without untying any of the points; but they annoyed me at the time, and it cost me a good deal of trouble to mend the mainsail and the windlass. But in the highest degree annoying was the fact that none of them ever made any suggestion of their own initiative except to ask me to shorten sail; it was a good thing they had not enough initiative to shorten sail themselves, or we should never have got anywhere. And very often I had to comply, for there were some wonderfully bad helmsmen among them, and I dislike the thought of being drowned. To most of them I am sure it never occurred that they might get drowned too if they were careless; they seemed to think that I had a magical property of getting them out of trouble.

They came on board either to get more wages and comfort than they would have elsewhere, or to get from one colony to another where they were not so well known; and after all why else should anyone go to sea? I was probably lucky in finding two really good men out of sixteen.

If the crews I signed on in foreign ports took it for granted that I was going yachting, the Port and other Authorities often acted on the assumption that mine was an ordinary trading vessel, sometimes to the extent of quite unreasonable claims for dues. One cannot foretell how a Harbour Board is going to treat a yacht flying the Blue Ensign, and it is no more use stereotyping advice or warning about these things than about the soundings in the Hugli River. But I think it is permissible for me to warn visiting yachtsmen of what they may expect to the extent of observing that on the other side of the world the man in the street, perhaps because he takes far more interest in his merchant shipping than we do at home, takes far less interest in his yachts and his yacht clubs. The latter therefore cannot give the visitor the facilities he enjoys in our ports; and the man in the street never puts himself into a punt and comes out to offer his services, or even to sell them, or anything else, at sea price. Heaven help anyone who enters in distress those raw countries the inhabitants of which pride themselves on their independence. I do not now wonder at the premium the insurance companies wanted for purely harbour risks.

It is obviously impossible to thank individually all the people that helped me on my way; it would be invidious to thank some; *qui palmam meruit, ferat*. But I must pay this tribute to the honesty of the world at

34

large. I never locked up anything and I never lost anything except to two persons, notorious bad characters,
who had been sent down to join the ship from the
Mercantile Marine offices of their respective ports.

Under these conditions I made a voyage, as the Ship's
Articles put it, "to any part of the world, terminating
. . . within two years"; and so unlucky, or so unwise
was I in dealing with the problems that faced me in
nearly every port that I finished up with a race against
time to get home within those two years. But every long
passage is in a sense a race, a race against the consumption of stores; and even if one had unlimited stores
it would still be a race against boredom; the only way
to keep one's interest alive is to indulge in experiments
with sails and rigging and speculations about the Laws
of Storms. Because therefore the physical facts of wind
and sea are very real to me, and because their record
may be of use to other yachtsmen, I have given them a
space which I hope will satisfy the legitimate curiosity
of the professed seaman without proving excessive for
the taste of the general public; somewhat, it may be, to
the exclusion of the generally unsatisfactory human
element.

Let it not be supposed, however, that this voyage
was unmitigated calamity, though had I known how
troublesome it would be I should have turned back
from Africa, and I tried hard to sell the ship in New
Zealand. On the whole it was worth while; there are
not so many adventures offering nowadays that one can
afford to miss even a modest one; and if the adventure
of one's choice leads across oceans there are not many
ways of spending tolerably six weeks out of the sight of
land. To us in a small boat our way is more than

tolerable; it is fascinating to study the infinitely varying forms of deep-sea waves. Now we float lazily among long round-backed hills, once in a while rising to a higher summit from which we can look down on a level horizon deep blue beneath a tropic sun; now we fight our way through ranges of snow-capped peaks, flanked by sharp-crested spurs that rise and burst with volcanic energy along our rail; and again we dance along the ridges and furrows rippled before the mild Trade Wind.

The features which can hardly be appreciated from the boat-deck of a liner rise up like a mountain-chain against the sky from our low view-point; only in our tiny craft can one feel the glorious back and forward swing of the racing seas. The transparency of the thin wall which is just about to break in a sparkle of sunlit foam, the minute tracery on the front of an advancing swell, are only enjoyed by an eye that is below their own level. And the myriad reflected lights from sunset clouds, which keep their distance from the more exalted observer, crowd close along our side that rises but two feet out of the water.

Perhaps I have been betrayed by the proximity of the sea into overestimating its height and steepness, or by the insignificance of my yacht into exaggerating the force of the wind, or by all of these into attaching an undue importance to storm sailing; but in these matters I have tried to be as accurate as I can, for the benefit of any reader who may imagine that this is a textbook of Ocean Yachting; and I hope he will be able to believe what I have written. I have no such hope of the general reader, to whom truth is less credible than fiction; for I have not confirmed my tale with miracles, but documented it with the bald and unconvincing statements of the Admiralty Sailing Directions. Who would believe that humming-birds suck the flowers of Staten Island—the next land to Cape Horn? Who would believe that the Government pilot at French Pass was not a man but a porpoise? Who would believe in penguins, unless he had seen them? Who, in short, will believe the plain story which begins on the next page of this book?

CHAPTER II

CROSSING THE ATLANTIC

THE crew that signed on in Dublin were not entirely strange to the ship, for, as one of them was used to big square-riggers and the other to small boats, I stipulated that they should sail round from the Shannon to Dunleary with me to see if they could survive a 20-tonner. This was the only trial trip I was able to make during the two years; and I do not think trial trips are much use anyway. The Captain is inclined to make too much allowance for strange surroundings, and the crew are inclined to be too much on their good behaviour. It is particularly difficult to tell how things are going to work out when one starts, as we did, on a yachting basis, and when one cannot detach oneself and look at the ship from outside. My crew got some idea of how to handle the boat, but I got very little idea of how to handle them. The weather, however, played its part to perfection; Providence, observing that we were clothed and equipped for a summer cruise round the coast, sent us a north-easterly gale in the Irish Sea, with a temperature of 35° Fahrenheit. We were never likely to meet such unpleasant weather again, and all hands signed on; so I was made easy on one score.

As a contrast, when I let go my moorings at 4.30 p.m. on the 20th of June, 1923, conditions were extraordinarily favourable. I wanted them to be so. This was my first essay at provisioning a ship for a long voyage: a long voyage, forsooth, when we expected to be at Madeira in a fortnight! Looking back on the fearful scenes enacted in Dunleary in that month of June I think I must have laid in stores for six months at least. Some of them were still extant after two years. But I was not the only offender. My mate H., a person of more charm than discretion, had collected in three weeks an amazing amount of impedimenta; my A.B. acting as cook and steward (a not uncommon rating in small craft) brought down mountainous contributions from benefactors whose identity for the most part I never discovered, and annexed, quite unwittingly, a cold chicken belonging to someone else's luncheon party and a live but microscopic black kitten. The chicken was a godsend. We really had not time both to cook dinner and to clear up the mess on deck before nightfall, fine though the weather was. And when we had stowed below all the things that should go below, there was left a semi-permanent deck cargo the very thought of which now appals me. There was, in addition to the spare spars, oars, boat-hooks, and so forth to be expected on any yacht's deck, one boat, canvas, fortunately folding, one sea anchor complete, two drums of oil to pour on the troubled waters, two 10-gallon breakers; three sacks of vegetables, three sacks of coal (imagine the lunacy of carrying a deck cargo of coal through the Tropics), four . . . But enough; and yet more is to come. On top of all one yard, 22 feet long, to which is bent some 80 running yards of No. 4 canvas, together with lifts, braces, inhauls, outhauls; we had not then discovered that the proper place for a yard is across the mast. It was a fine night with a smooth sea, and at noon next day we took our departure from the Tuskar, and settled into sea routine. "We" here, and until my arrival at Durban, includes H., for he navigated the ship with diligence, sailed her with enthusiasm, and alone made it possible for me to start. I think that to the ideal captain of a small yacht he would be an ideal mate; but alas! I am not an ideal captain.

We were lucky in getting gentle N.N.W. breezes after clearing the land, freshening by degrees, but not so much as to prevent our making all the westing we wanted. The third night out indeed it seemed to me to be distinctly fresh, with a pretty rough beam sea, but in those early days I used to be scared of every puff of wind, and wake up wondering what the other fellow was doing with the ship, and whether the ship was going to hold together. Not until I had been out for three months did I feel sure that the ship was all right, and assume that the other fellow had no more desire to drown himself than to drown me, and acquire the art of sleeping through any gale. I really took things ridiculously seriously; even after two years I connect my passage down the Atlantic with nothing else but anxious readings of the barometer and thermometer, and speculations about wind and weather; I cannot get away from the navigational problems and play with situations as I did on the homeward voyage.

That was the final kick of the miserably cold and stormy early summer from which we had suffered in Dublin; the next day we ran into real summer. In lat. 49° N. and long. 10° W. we got the Portuguese Trades and knew we should have a fair wind for the next 2,500 miles; with indeed a chance of a day or two of calm in the middle of that distance, but with the knowledge that the breeze would be constant in direction and for the most part just the strength we wanted it. It certainly began very light, but the sea had become glassy smooth and the ship was gliding along at 5 knots right before the wind. We sent up the foreyard and set the foresail, lashed the wheel, fed the kitten, of whose life we had despaired, on sardines, as she would not touch condensed milk, and disposed ourselves to sleep on the shadier parts of the deck. It is not always that the yacht will steer herself with both square and fore-and-aft canvas set; for when she starts rolling she shakes the wind out of the mainsail, and the foresail, being less affected, pulls her head round. But at that time, with her original mast, she would generally look after herself for a considerable time; it was considered a great hardship if we could not all sit down to dinner together. This afternoon it was my wheel, a fact which I recognized suitably by going to sleep; but not in the shade, whereby I burned most of the skin off my bac . It is necessary, however, to lose a skin or two in order to become sun-proof, a very convenient quality when one can only wash one's clothes after a heavy shower of rain. It was interesting to observe that whereas the mate and I never wore hats, or indeed anything else except for the sake of warmth, and the third hand never went on deck without a red flannel shirt and a green umbrella, he was the only one on board who complained of the heat. Strange that one should babble about Trade Winds and green umbrellas here, three days out from Dublin and 1,500 miles from the Tropic of Cancer! It shows how small the world is, and how readily anyone that has a boat can exchange the cold grey of our coast for the sapphires and diamonds of the south.

The good north-east wind held steady, freshening day

by day; the blue seas rolled up astern, each day steeper and with a heavier crest of white; the foam lapped over in the waist and hissed along the rail to the bows; and our wake showed green farther and farther astern. That foam that lapped over the waist found out one of our weaknesses; just there was the galley skylight, and just abaft the skylight was the mainsheet; and on occasions of injudicious gybing bights of the mainsheet had more than once got round that skylight and had lifted it off its coamings. And what looked like foam on deck proved to be green water in the galley. Now I had designed that galley with great consideration for light and air, and with a head wind and sea, which at home is the time one gets wettest, it is in the driest part of the ship. But we were going to run with the wind aft for weeks at a time, and I had put that galley in the wettest part of a running ship; and just now I was running her. With little effort she did 160 and then 170 miles in the day, the mate sitting on the taffrail playing the mandolin and steering with one foot, the third hand foolishly trailing a line over the stern in quest of fish. I say foolishly, because I find that he trailed that line for about 6,700 miles and caught four fish on it; that is one to every 1,675 miles, or less frequently than once a fortnight. I told him there was more than a possibility of an accidental gybe, as the ship was rolling badly and the wind was unsteady; and sure enough, while it was my wheel, the gybe came, and the mizzen-sheet caught my unfortunate fisherman and gave him concussion of the brain. Four months later I thought: "It was my wheel; I tried to kill him but failed"; but at the time I was not convinced of the justification for murder, and set to reducing canvas so that the mate and I could both bear a hand to get him below. And this meant first of all taking in the foresail, which I proceeded to do, while the mate steered. In those days there was no gear on the foresail, which travelled on hoops on the yard, except the inhauls and outhauls; consequently when one had hauled in the head one had to get the whole contraption down on deck, keeping the inhauls taut and muzzling the sail with one hand while one lowered away on the halliards with the other. In ten minutes I thought out half-a-dozen better ways of doing the job. Without the foresail two of us could do anything with the ship; the wind and sea went down, the patient improved, and we got on with our voyage towards Madeira.

Next day the wind fell very light, and the mate and I were busy shifting sails. There had been a possibility of heavy weather on the coast, so we had left home with the new suit bent; besides it looked better, for the old sails were very patched and parti-coloured. There was nothing else to do this day, and we did not want to leave the work to be done at Madeira, where we were going to amuse ourselves. Those sails were not only very patched but they were very old. The jib was made by Ratsey, but some twenty years ago; the mainsail, a much better setting sail than the new one, only twelve, but one of them was spent covering a hayrick. The rest were good enough for a steady following breeze, but would probably blow away in the South-East Trades. While we were bending them our patient sat up and took an interest in turtle, which we could not catch, but which were a pleasant reminder that we were approaching tropical seas. This was the only time we saw them, and in those days we kept a good look-out for birds and beasts. These seas, however, did not seem a very good hunting ground for the naturalist; beyond shoals of leaping squid and a number of birds which looked like skuas and were apparently after the squid, there was nothing conspicuous. But there were some very beautiful small jelly-fishes, marked with a cross-pattern of iridescent scales; and a small fleet of Portuguese men-of-war.

Meanwhile we had lost the Portuguese Trades and did not get the genuine article for two days, and when it came, on the 2nd of July, it was very light. But it was enough to give us flying-fish for breakfast, and a sight of Porto Santo Island after breakfast. Porto Santo is not, as these things go, a very exciting example of an oceanic island, for it is of no great elevation; but it was the first I had seen, and I saw it in a leisurely manner and from a short distance; and it struck me forcibly as being like nothing so much as a kaolin dump overrun by the washings of a tin mine. Of course there must be rock on it, but if the adjacent island of Madeira is any criterion, it must be singularly rotten rock; and there must be cultivation on it, for the best Madeira wine is grown there; and I suppose it is not really all red and white except to people whose eyes have been supersensitized by the endless blue of sea and sky.

Knight, in his *Cruise of the " Falcon,"* has described the approach to Funchal. I cannot improve on his language without becoming blasphemous. It was after breakfast next morning when I got my pilot. I like to employ a pilot, even for an open anchorage such as this, since it is his funeral if I get foul of the quarantine regulations. But I employ him as pilot; my third hand, in his capacity of steward, employed him, unknown to me, as caterer; and next morning I was faced with a boat-load of fruit and vegetables sufficient for a mail-steamer, and a bill in proportion. With some difficulty I succeeded in bribing him to take the stuff away, and I severely reprimanded my steward; if I had possessed the gift of prophecy I should have taken advantage of a homeward-bound mail-steamer lying alongside of us.

After three days and a shore adventure which was the most dangerous experience of the voyage, but about which diplomatic reasons enjoin silence, I thought it prudent to get to sea again.

But first of all I had to get a sea rate for my chrono-meter; and this I got from a very fantastic steam yacht that came in that morning, the "F" of Liverpool. Now my chronometer was, according to the makers, showing Greenwich time when I left Dublin; according to a young gentleman in an optician's shop it was twenty-eight seconds slow. At Funchal it was seven seconds slow. Knowing the casual nature of young gentlemen in opticians' shops I disregarded his version and logged the rate as half a second a day losing. The navigating officer of the "F" gave us the signal with a revolver; when I came to know more about his crew I wondered that revolver had not been used on us in another way, for many of the "F's" were ex-Auxiliaries or Black and Tans, and we were flying a large tricolour. It was lucky he did not use it as a target, for we were already getting rather short of bunting. We could not buy a Portuguese flag; no shop will stock the Red and Green of their Republic when the ensign may to-morrow be again White and Blue of the Monarchy; and we had to trade one of our tricolours with the "V," the British Consul's little ketch, for a very shabby rag of hers.

The object of this deal in bunting appeared when we did get away, for the "V" escorted us out of the bay flying our tricolour at the fore, while we reciprocated with his ensign; somewhat to the bewilderment of sundry good folk of Funchal, who, the wish being father to the thought, imagined the Green, White, and Orange to be the colours of an independent Republic of Madeira. Months afterwards, when people commented on the raggedness of my ensign, it sounded well to say, "Oh, I had to lend my best one to So-and-so; he was Acting-Consul for Ireland at Madeira."

So I entered and left my first foreign port, having, I hope, behaved with propriety therein. I knew that Consuls expected their existence to be recognized, but did not want trivial formalities; that the spending of a few milreis on a national flag on one's arrival is much appreciated, and of a few more on rockets on one's departure still more so; and that one should never buy anything oneself or by one's crew, but do all one's business through an agent.

It was six in the evening of the 6th of July when we got under way, with the lightest of airs, in which we were able to sail round the " V "; and all that night was a virtual calm, but fortunately not troubled by such an abominable sea as marred the calm of our entry to Funchal. Yet the island, at first a network of spangled lines, like a spider's web under a dewy moon, gradually faded to a dark purple patch shimmering with fluorescent light, and by dawn was invisible. As we drew slowly away from the land the wind revived (islands, especially near the limits of the Trades, are a perfect curse) and we knew that there was nothing to do but to sit down and look at the ship being blown along to St.

Vincent. I think we rather overdid the sitting down, and would have been better employed taking in the gaff-topsail; for off the Canary Islands, which we gave a berth of some 30 miles, the wind was blowing half a gale at times and there was a mighty rough irregular sea. H., the mate, thought the ship was doing 9 knots, and would run 200 miles in the 24 hours. No doubt she did 9 knots when we brought the wind well out on the quarter; but no two men could steer her like that, watch and watch for 24 hours, for she was going mad altogether; even running dead before the wind, which slowed her down to 7 knots, I had all I wanted. In those days the helmsman had none of our modern conveniences. He had a most uncomfortable and cramped way of steering, sitting forward of and to one side of the wheel. He had no way of calling his relief except by lashing the wheel and crawling forward to hammer on the deck. I made it noon of the 9th of July, noted with disgust that we had only run 185 miles, and lost no time getting the gaff-topsail in. The log subsequently contains an entry, "Thank God for a quiet night after yesterday's carry on "; and a run of 155 miles. It is easy to be wise after the event; but I think that if we had not carried that topsail the first day, but set it the second, we should have made runs of 190 and 170 miles respectively. But to make good runs in such conditions one wants three helmsmen; even my indefatigable mate admitted as much. Yet we kept on with two watches till after the Cape Verde Islands.

In another respect I now found out that my new yacht worked one hand harder than was necessary, or at least than my old yacht. I made a swinging table in the saloon, and thought that by its means the

steward would always have a level place to put down a
dish on. With a properly constructed and ballasted table
this is so; my old yacht never threw anything off hers.
But this one, in certain conditions of wind and sea,
starts swinging so violently that nothing at all will stay
on it. I have tried to control it with springs, with less
ballast, with weights on the sides; all to little effect. It
takes two to lay dinner; that is, one to lay it and the
other to hold on to the table, when it starts its antics.

Hereabouts we indulged in speculations about submarine volcanic action. On the evening of the 10th the
sun was an unnatural pale yellow and the sky a dirty
grey; early next morning, in about lat. 22° 30° N. and
long. 19° 20° W., two very heavy seas broke on board;
at daylight the water looked like black mud. Probably
the first phenomena were due to a Harmattan; ab-
normal seas are not always caused by earthquakes; and
discoloured water is always reported in this neighbourhood. I remarked that this was the only night on which
I saw any considerable amount of phosphorescence in
the water. Here, as well as the seas, the largest flying-
fish I ever saw came on board; he was 14½ inches long
and 16½ across the wings.

Since passing the Canaries we had not had at all my
idea of Trade Wind weather. The sky had been dull and
cloudy, though no rain had fallen; the wind had been
fresh and puffy, and there had been a very big swell
coming in from the eastward all the time. This latter
did not inconvenience us much as long as the wind held,
but when on the 12th it fell very light, we had to take
in the mainsail to save our gear and roll along under
foresail only to the westward, to bring the swell astern.

So far I have made no reference to navigation and

very little to the trimming of sail. It might be supposed that, like a steamboat captain, I just set courses and got to the end of them; and in a way this is very nearly true. A steamboat small enough to be comparable with my yacht would not have made very different courses; and they would not have been Mercator courses or great circle courses or any definite sort of courses, but those which are dictated by the wind and still more by the sea. Why a steamboat as well as a sailing vessel goes slowest with wind and sea right aft is an unanswerable question; but to the captain of a small vessel it is an academic question, since he has to keep them so for the sake of safety and comfort. If I can show a straight week's run it is the fortuitous resultant of a hundred varying courses, and almost certainly postulates slight or moderate seas. My track down the North Atlantic makes an ugly but economical line.

As the ship would steer herself all right under the present canvas we all turned in for the night, having made an entry in the log to the effect that the lights were burning brightly. It was not true, which was very wrong, because we were well in the track of steamers. Homeward bounders at first; these did not confirm my position, about which I was beginning to have doubts, for they might have called at S. Vincent for bunkers. But in time an outward-bound vessel, obviously not a collier, passed east of us; by no possibility could she have been going between the islands, and we must have been miles out in our reckoning. We cast back to the eastwards, steering for the dirtiest-looking part of the horizon; for it is notorious that the Cape Verde Islands are perpetually shrouded in mists.

The tropic night closed down while I was waiting to

get a sight of Jupiter on the meridian; here sights for
latitude have to be taken within a very small margin of
time, and in this atmosphere only the larger planets
were visible; but I was sufficiently reassured to set the
ship head-reaching to the eastward with the probability
of seeing the light on Sant' Antão before midnight and
a certainty of being in position to run in for the channel
at daylight. The place was thick with steamers and it
was as black as pitch, so I did not spare carbide; and the
result was extremely picturesque. The brilliant jet of
acetylene in the saloon threw the shadows of the rods
of the skylight all over the gleaming sails like the ribs of
a huge fan which was white to port, where the light fell
on the foresail, and reddish to starboard over the tanned
mainsail; and on the clew of the foresail a rosy tint, and
on that of the mainsail a whitish green, where the beams
from the sidelights caught them. You can't see all this
in most yachts, because they have ground or otherwise
obscured glass in their skylights, a thing which I do
not like, for it makes the cabins dark and it prevents
one from seeing the weather-vane at the truck from
one's seat at the dinner table.

All these steamers which we saw this night had pre-
sumably been buying coal at sea-price from the various
emporia of S. Vincent. When we were leaving the
Islands the Captain of a Welsh collier bound to Cape
Town in ballast remarked that we should be sailing in
company; "For," said he, "if the South-East Trade
comes away strong, a light ship like this ought to take
advantage of the Brazilian monsoon, and then slip
across in the westerlies, as you will." And the moral of
that is that a man with a knowledge of the winds even
in a steamboat will save his owners' coal (what if he is

a Welshman?), while the men that steam about at haphazard have to bunker at exorbitant rates.

There are only two hours in the day when these islands are on show; at daybreak when the stupendous cliffs of Sant' Antão rise in 7,000 feet of golden fire against the retreating night clouds, and at dusk when they stand a jagged purple barrier against the evanescent sunset; for the rest they are hidden in the eternal haze that envelops the land. So we, coming in with the sunrise, saw the shore at its best, and before it had faded had turned our attention in the other direction, to S. Vincent, and were looking for a berth in the harbour of Porto Grande. I do not include S. Vincent among the æsthetic attractions of the islands, for it is merely grotesque, a piece of unmitigated desert set up on the edge and finished off by the pantomime scene-painter to represent the Ogre's Fastness. On it there are two trees, and why there should be so many is a mystery; there is no water, except what is brought from Tarafal, 10 miles away on Sant' Antão; there is no grass; I believe the local golf links to be continuous bunkers interspersed with concrete putting greens. It lives on contraband, cable companies, and coal—principally coal; and I saw more coal than I wanted. For the unlucky P., whom I had prevented from buying things, must slip off while I was busy with customs and police formalities and introduce himself, and by implication the ship, to certain coal merchants whom I did not wish to meet, to the exclusion of the cable-station crowd whom I did. But I called upon them later, since, as I had very nearly missed the islands altogether, it was most important that I should know whether it was my navigation or my chronometer that was at fault. It was the latter, or rather my interpretation of it; for the casual-looking young gentleman in Dublin was right, and the makers in London were wrong. I had subsequently no trouble from the instrument.

The time unfortunately was not ripe for revising my crew list, for S. Vincent was the last place where I had any chance of picking up a sailor till I got to Polynesia; but I did not of course know at the time that sailors have ceased to exist except in such out-of-the-way places as this. Of the few survivors the Portuguese islanders are probably the best, though the younger generation are only schooner men since the New Bedford whaling fleet disappeared. I could have got first-class men here, for one of their smartest rum-runners had just been lost, and there was rather a slump in the contraband trade; and also one or two of the smaller islands had been abandoned owing to the fact that no rain had fallen for four years; so there was a certain amount of unemployment. As the weather was very hot —this was the only place I really felt the heat except for an hour or so in Durban when a northerly wind was blowing; and that was very soon counteracted by a bitter south-west gale—I turned two of the unemployed on to unbending and stowing away the foresail and all its gear. It was not worth while to keep it for a rather problematical two days of Trade Winds, and once we got into the Doldrums everything would be soaked and we could not put it below in the sail-room. I believe in the square rig for any ocean-going vessel however small except in two sets of circumstances: in squally weather, when it might be dangerous to be taken aback; and where one expected a long spell of head winds and wanted to lessen the resistance of the extra gear as much as possible. And there lay before us first a belt of calms with squalls, and then a wider belt of head winds in the South-East Trade.

On the evening of the 18th of July we weighed and ran through the S. Vincent channel with a nice breeze. It is to be observed that one wants a nice breeze, for a most unexpected current sets to windward through it; and that is probably the reason why when the wind dropped at nightfall we seemed to stop there or thereabouts. Where "there" was, I have not the slightest idea; all night was pitchy black, and in the morning I could not see 3 miles; and so it went on for two days. We could not have been far from the land, for we were invaded by butterflies and the like; *Pyrameis Cardui*, *Plusia Bractea* (or a near relative) and innumerable dragon-flies.

The whole atmosphere was depressing; perhaps the gilt had worn rather thin on the gingerbread with too much hard work, for both H. and I were, unknown to each other, regretting that we had started on a basis of two watches. P. was much distressed because when he dug out his shore-going clothes he found them coagulated into a solid mass of mildew; but he bred mildews. I foresaw in the near future a time when there would be nothing left on board except the horrid meats that are in tins; not even the kind of biscuits that are in tins, for some perverse person had lost or broken the lids of all of them, and the resultant moulds had invaded all my lockers in general and my crocks of butter in particular. Some of the stores were hauled on deck to dry; ten pounds of candles to wit, which exposed to a tropical sun were no doubt very good for the deck, but disappointing to anyone that wanted candles. If these things happen in the comparatively dry air of the Trades, what will happen in the green atmosphere of the Doldrums? Only the kitten was contented with life. She had been weaned from sardines to a diet of flying-fish, much to her disgust, but her tastes were too expensive; she was swelling visibly.

The watch-keeping problem settled itself on the second night. I, not realizing how chilly a tropical shower could be, had gone to bed with a temperature of 102. I ought to have kept the middle watch, but P. had to do it for me. When I came on deck at 4 a.m. I informed him that this arrangement would be permanent.

There was never more than a ghost of the North-East Trade beyond the Islands, and we had lost nothing by sending down the foreyard. I learned from steamers that the South-East Trade extended to lat. 5° N. and that there had been southerly winds from there on.

The sea was full of flying-fish, and as it was so smooth one could observe them with some facility from the lee bow, or from an even better point of vantage, the bob-stay, and thus get them against the sky where they are far more visible than against the water, the tone of which they imitate closely. I am prepared to swear that they can and do fly, all the statements of the anatomists notwithstanding. At least I say that by vibrating their wings they can increase their height and their speed and make abrupt turns in circumstances which preclude the hypothesis of an ascending puff of wind under them. But they cannot rise from the deck, and they are very good eating. This last opinion is shared by the dolphin, the *coryphæna*, that is, the dolphin of the seaman, who was hot in their pursuit but curiously enough turned aside to investigate a piece of white rag with a hook in it. He was even better eating. It is no fable about the changing colours of the dying dolphin; the colours indeed are more beautiful when he is alive, but they are more permanent.

The past couple of days the flying-jib had been set, and not before it was time, for, being a cotton sail, it was a mass of mildew; but very much to the annoyance of the cat and to our anxiety. She fortunately could not climb the rigging—which is the foolish habit of ships' cats, for they cannot get down again—for my shrouds were not served over and her claws got no grip on the bare wire; but she used to promenade along the jib-boom. This was all right when she had the flying-jib sheets and downhaul to hold on to on the way out, and the soft canvas of the sail to turn round on; on the morning of the 24th of July she was not to be found, and it is supposed that she slipped off the naked varnished spar. This sad accident left a great gap in the community; and yet I don't know why I should feel the loss of a cat, for she was an undeniable nuisance. But cats would be the best kind of sea-going stock if it were not for their inconvenient love of exploration; they are so cosy in repose, and in action so independent and unconscious of the movement of the ship.

On the next day we lost the Trade Wind, in lat. 10° 20′ N., and were left anxiously wondering what would come next. We had come to a region where (I quote from memory) calms alternate with tremendous squalls accompanied by torrential rain and lightning, where waterspouts and tornadoes pursue the vessel and the tormented sea rises in a confused swell that hurls the yards off the masts, while the hot damp air breeds fevers till those that do not die have no longer strength to work the ship. Much of this I discounted, for if one paid any attention to the Sailing Directions one would never dare to go to sea at all. We started with one of the calms; but by midnight a light but steady westerly air had set us slipping easily over a glassy sea. At daylight the gaff-topsail was stowed and shortly afterwards a reef put in the mainsail as the wind freshened but without altering its direction. For some two hours we had the conditions for which we always prayed, a strong breeze on the beam and a smooth sea. The water boiled in the lee scuppers as we dragged our rail down to it, but for a time so little spray came over from windward that it did not interfere with laundry operations on that side of the deck; for it rained. No one, I regret to say, had the curiosity to take the temperature of the fresh water; that of the sea was 83°, and it was a surprising sensation to step over from one side of the deck to the other, but by degrees the water was warmed and the soap-suds curdled and then washed away by the ever-increasing volume of spray that came over, while our speed dropped from a dizzy 9 knots to a labouring 7 as the wind and sea came on our bow; and then by noon both wind and sea had gone and yet we were still drifting—though not I am sure by any virtue of the sails, which hung up and down as stiff as boiler-plate with the wet which under that cloudy sky showed no signs of running out of them—drifting somehow to the southward. If there were going to be no more weight than that in the squalls, and if the sea remained smooth, we could luff through them till we gauged their force and the amount of sail we could safely carry—a manœuvre of which I do not, however, at all approve if there is any sea—so I turned the reef out of the mainsail for the rest of the

Doldrums. But this first day was not a fair sample of Doldrum weather. The next was fine and sunny till late afternoon, with no rain, and enough wind to give us 75 miles of southing; not bad for the latitude and time of year. It also provided us with a little excitement in the form of two small sperm whales, with one of which we narrowly escaped a collision. I had gone out on the jib-boom to try to get a photograph of him, but at the critical moment I was far too much occupied in securing a line of retreat in case he struck us, when I presume he would have cut off the boom with his tail, to use the camera. He seemed to be entirely unconscious of the ship; they say these whales cannot see anything right ahead of them, and it just happened that instead of hitting us he dived under our forefoot, much to the alarm of our pilot-fish. The pilot-fish was not designed to have business with ships; he does not guide them, indeed, if the expression is permitted, he follows them six inches in advance. If your ship is going slowly enough you will see the little fellow, the dark stripes on his back showing up finely against the blue depths, so apparently immovable that you think he is in some way attached to the stem; in fine weather he will travel thus for days, and how he gets his sleep or his food is a mystery. But all the time he is looking for a shark, for a shark is his business; he is only working a passage on your ship. The articles of association are these. The pilot-fish undertakes to find food, and try if it is wholesome, or if there is a hook buried in it, for the shark is very short-sighted; the shark provides protection and transport. On a passage, when the pilot-fish gets sleepy, he turns in inside the shark's mouth. This pilot-fish is on no account to be confused with Pelorus Jack, who was recognized by an Act of the New Zealand Parliament as the pilot at French Pass; he was not a fish in the proper sense, but a porpoise.

The third day of Doldrums was fine and sunny with a couple of showers.

On the morning of the fourth it rained. In the evening a steady fresh southerly wind sprang up; before dark we had the gaff-topsail stowed and a reef in the mainsail, and were plunging into a rising sea. Wherever we were, we were out of the Doldrums, without seeing any waterspouts (though one cloud looked hopefully bulgy) or any other amusing phenomena.

Opinions differ as to whether this was the South-East Trade or the South-West Monsoon; I believe they are continuous, and we were just where the one turns into the other. On the 29th of July in lat. 7° N. I got on the port tack, and though the wind stayed continuously southerly I made a very good course through the kind offices of the Guinea Current. Two days later I made a very bad mistake. The sea was getting rather rough, the wind was veering a little, and I was afraid we were running out of our friendly current and into a foul one, so I tacked again. Certainly we went faster and drier, but Lord! what a course! And very soon the sea was worse than ever. On the 2nd of August, in lat. 3½° N. and long. 19½° W., I got on the proper tack again, and felt quite sure about the authenticity of the Trade Wind. I had wasted at least a day by that deplorable tack. Now, however, the sea became smooth and we, sailing 6 knots on a bowline, crossed the Equator in long. 22° W. very early in the morning of the 5th.

The sensible Equator, however, is not the straight line round the earth in lat. 0°, as the geographers would have it; over that one can sail without experiencing the least shock, for it is only a matter of applying certain arithmetical formulæ, of which the values change imperceptibly, to the culmination of certain heavenly bodies. One hardly notices the shifting or the disappearance of familiar landmarks; imperceptibly Merak and Dubhe cease to point to the Pole Star; but quite startlingly some night the Centaurs call attention to the Southern Cross, and to the fact that one is in southern seas. So also the world seems suddenly turned upside down when the sun at noon is to the North—and that may happen 1,400 miles from the true Equator. It took me some little time to get accustomed to seeing the stars moving the wrong way—I have to a considerable extent an absolute sense of direction, and never felt the ship was sailing the wrong way—to carrying my anchor on the starboard bow, and to finding the wind always backing. I might explain that the meteorologists have recently agreed to use the word "veering" of winds shifting with the hands of the clock, and "backing" for the reverse, in either hemisphere.

Here we had broken the back of the passage to the Cape eleven days from the time we had lost the North-East Trade, and I do not think I had steered the most judicious courses through this, the most controversial area of the oceans. It would appear that the Doldrums are not a belt of calm extending the whole way across the Atlantic, but that, at certain times of the year at any rate, they do not exist to the westward of the 30th Meridian—in April 1925 there were no Doldrums in $30\frac{1}{2}°$ W.—and eastward of the 20th they are replaced by the Guinea Monsoon. In the latter there is plenty of wind, but a head wind, and an abominable sea; the middle course—the recommended course—is a calm and vexatious compromise; when next I go that way I shall keep to the westward and take the risk of getting to leeward of the Brazilian coast.

I confess that with all my preliminary study of charts I had not at all realized how narrow in the middle the Atlantic Ocean is; or perhaps rather with what generous sweeps one is expected to wander down it by the authors of the *Africa Pilot*, one of the most delightfully informative books I know, when they warn one against getting set on to Cape San Roque. What a breadth of view as to the limits of Africa that shows! One might suppose that the passage to the Cape was more or less of a coasting voyage, and that a ship was extravagantly taking both sides of the ocean if the Atlantic was not wide enough for her; but as a matter of fact we, taking a much more easterly route than most sailing vessels do, found ourselves very much nearer the Brazilian than the Guinea coast when the accident occurred which compelled us to go looking for a harbour.

In the wonderful smooth seas of these three days we had performed, for the first and only time, the laborious operation of transferring 50 gallons of water from our forward tank, which stood by itself, to the main tank, which was connected to the pantry pump. It all had to be dipped out through a handhole—providentially a Bath Oliver biscuit tin would just fit—handed up on deck, and poured through the ordinary filling pipe. Another connexion to the pump was the first item on my defect list for the next refit. We also hauled most of the things that were below up on deck, and found to our amazement that the mildews were wilting away and that things were very much drier and cleaner than they had been. And there was a moral as well as a material improvement about the ship, even before Neptune in person came on board to give the crew encouragement and their certificates. We crossed the Line at the unconscionable hour of 1.30 a.m. Neptune likes promptness, but at present rates cannot afford to pay his bears, barbers, and policemen over-time; he, therefore, came unattended. But H., who had met his Majesty before, had decorated the saloon and laid the Sword and Mace and scrolls of parchment in readiness for him. I admire the staging of the affair as much as I treasure the document which gives me the Freedom of the Seas. As for dinner that night, shall I ever forget it? Yachting is yachting on the 5th of August, whether in Cowes or one degree south of the Line. I may have been cheered up by that dinner, or by the relief with which I discovered that the South-East Trade did not blow, as all reports insisted, much harder than the North-East; but I wrote down—for in those early and enthusiastic days I wrote down a number of foolish things—that there was a new heaven not only where the constellations came upside down across the sky but also on my ship. Fortunately for themselves, men have not the gift of prophecy.

Next day I noticed that the mast-head was very crooked, and, disregarding a not very serious-looking rent, we hove-to and got it tolerably straight by setting up the rigging. And while we were hove-to, we put the boat over the side, and attacked a luxuriant growth of barnacles with a long-handled scraper, but without entire success; and located a small leak—for having once owned a really unseaworthy yacht I had not quite got over the feeling on a breezy night that we might go

down all at once—as due to a defective seam and of no
importance. And while the boat was there I sent H.
away with his camera to immortalize us. These things
are not commonly done in mid-ocean. But the weather,
though never up to the ferocity of that we met off the
Canary Islands—and who says now that the South-East
Trade in the Atlantic is the surer of the two?—became
rather squally that night, and at dawn I saw the mast
was very much more crooked, and hung right over the
stern. I did not wait to call the other watch, but let go
the gaff-topsail and main halliards with a run. Then we
went aloft to investigate. The spar was split from some
5 feet below to the same distance above the hounds;
one could see daylight through the rent. After getting
lashings on it and wedging them up with great difficulty,
for the sea had now risen to a nasty little jobble, and the
ship rolled abominably, we found that we could safely
set the mainsail with two reefs in it. But under such a
jury rig we should be an age getting to the Cape; so we
bore away for Pernambuco, some 700 miles to leeward;
the very place which for the last ten days we had been
trying to avoid. It would not, however, delay us very
much, for we should get there on the day of the new
moon and might hope for a seven-foot tide and a chance
to get the rest of those barnacles off and start again with
a clean bottom.

The run in was very disappointing. The Trade Wind
was indeed the best of its kind that I fell in with, but it
was not good enough to give us more than 7 knots with
such a rig; and I only had four days' use of it, for on the
evening of the 11th I had to slow down and wait, in
company with two steamers, for daylight in order to
approach the harbour. On my homeward voyage I saw

other steamers in about the same place; between them I never saw any sort of vessel except when I could see land at the same time. The man that follows the old sailing routes in these days must have sound gear and plenty of stores, for the once frequented tracks are now a desert, and the crew of a ship that meets with an accident must depend on their own resources to get to port.

I had been a little uncertain about making the land at Pernambuco, since I was not yet quite sure of my chronometer; but I need have had no anxiety. As soon as it was dark we saw the blaze of the city lights some 50 miles away. At the appropriate time the mate went up to the mast-head to see Picão lighthouse; but between the sun on the top of the *Diario* building and the prodigality of electricity everywhere—this, observe, at half-past three in the morning—the lighthouse made a poor show. If any race is more lavish of street-lamps than the Portuguese, it is the Brazilians. But neither tolerate illuminated sky-signs such as disgrace our cities; if the orb on the dome of the *Diario* bears the name of that journal, it is so inconspicuous that I never noticed it.

At last the sun rose on the white palaces that line the whole water-front of Recife, and on the domes and towers of the churches which crowd the older quarters of the city. The captious may say that none of them are palaces, and that one indeed is the worst specimen of Wardour Street Gothic in existence. I do not care; this water-front gives such an overwhelming blow to the eye that one is blinded to the details. Let not any of us, who cannot even design details, throw stones.

I shall be expected to express poignant emotions at the discovery of the New World on the far side of an ocean which, a few months ago, seemed likely to put a bound to my travels; for I am by nature a very stay-at-home person and reluctant to leave my own parish. This is the result of laziness rather than of inability to adjust myself to a strange environment, for I am not at all frightened by finding myself in a foreign country, nor does the process of getting there savour of the miraculous. One loses a good deal by the matter-of-factness of modern travel; one loses in fact the ability to manufacture emotions on the occasion of one's first visit to America. This call at Pernambuco lacked interest because it was a possibility always contemplated; the only real discoveries are discoveries made by accident. But so well documented and charted was this voyage of mine that only once did I discover a place about which I knew nothing whatever, when I had to put in to Port Natal; once I deliberately refrained from reading up anything about the place I was going to (I was going as a passenger, and the sailing directions for Graham Land are not up to the standard of the *Africa Pilot* anyway) lest my impressions might be influenced by another's views on the subject; and one landfall gave me a real thrill, when I made Diego Ramirez after a week of imaginary dangers between the fiftieth parallel and the Horn. More things happened in the novitiate of our yachting, when we did not know where we were going to get to next, or indeed very precisely how we were going to get there. Failing my own, I thought I would try P.'s emotions, and I called him up on deck to see America. He looked over the side, saw that the water was like pale pea-soup instead of deep transparent blue, and all he said was, "My God, I didn't think it was as near as that!"

It is indeed shoal for a long way out, and there are some ugly reefs round the harbour entrance, but fortunately, as I had intended to call here on my way home, I had a good chart of the place. So after demonstrating for a time outside with a pilot signal I sailed inside the breakwater, and was boarded by the pilot, doctor, customs, police, and I know not who else, to all of whom I had the greatest difficulty in explaining why I had come to their port. Apparently none of them had yet heard that it was the most beautiful city in the world. But at the time I did not know that either; for, chafing at the unexpected delay, I was busy interviewing pilots, plumbers, engineers, carpenters, and all sorts of trades; for I had determined that I would not spend more than three days in Pernambuco.

CHAPTER III

TO THE EASTWARD

WE spent three weeks, not three days, in Pernambuco. With skill and foresight I had arranged to arrive on the day of the new moon, so as to get all the rise of tide available, and that was barely enough to beach the ship; for at that time the patent slip was dismantled and the dry dock was merely a sandbank in the middle of the harbour, which I examined that evening with one of the pilots. Unfortunately, next morning it was another pilot that came to take us up; in part it was the curse of Babel that got between us and caused us to miss that tide; in part it was, I fear, stupidity which impelled him to try to beach the yacht on a bank that sloped like the roof of a house; anyway, by the time I had got out of that predicament it was too late to get to the proper place. Next day some other curse fell upon us, and our crew turned up late. There was a noble tide this morning, but it was probably due to heavy rains up country, for there was a noble current as well, against which it was quite impossible for a four-oared-boat to tow us. Besides, the river was full of floating weeds, a sort of gigantic watercress, through which one could hardly row. They kept a man in the bows to cut through the tangles with a long-handled knife such as is called a "kelp-knife" in the Falkland Islands, where there is a worse, and an everyday problem, in the prodigious growths of seaweed. I would not risk the third day after

66

the moon, so there was a fortnight gone from us. However, I reckoned we should make most of it up by having a clean bottom. Meanwhile I turned my attention to the mast.

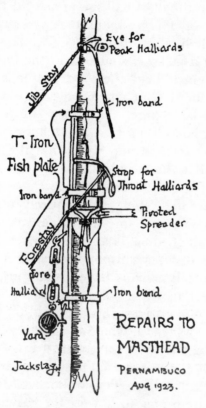

Eye for
Peak Halliards

Jib Stay

Iron band

T-Iron
Fish plate

Strop for
Throat Halliards

Iron band

Pivoted
Spreader

Forestay

Iron band

Fore
Halliard

REPAIRS TO
MASTHEAD
PERNAMBUCO
AUG 1923.

Yard

Jackstay

It was impossible to get a new spar in Pernambuco, but I got a very friendly and intelligent engineer to clamp 7 feet of T-iron as a fish-plate over the damaged part. I thought at the time that it would take me home, but it was not really satisfactory. Apart from the fact that if you mend a broken stick with an infinitely

67

strong patch which only extends a very short way over the sound part you are asking for another fracture at the end of it, the plate extended so far that I could not set my mainsail properly without a reef in it, which reduced my already small sail area, and I could not use a parrel for my foreyard, and that prevented my reefing the sail, which was rather large for a heavy gale. There was indeed a jackstay shackled to the lower end of the fish-plate which held the yard in place when it was hoisted right up, but when one lowered it, it was inclined to take charge. We unbent the tropical suit of sails, which had all survived, though the gaff-topsail had become so stretched and worn that it set like a flour-bag. Not that that would cause much comment here, for most of the local craft seem to use that material. And as they use fishing rods, entirely innocent of any stays, for spars, probably heavy canvas would not suit so well. Besides, their boats are so narrow and cranky the weight of proper sails might capsize them.

Indeed the Brazilians have great courage to go outside the reef in these contraptions, or on them (and let not anyone criticize this preposition, for there is no inside to a changada, which is merely a raft of six logs, fitted with a sail and centreboard), but they do go not only outside the reef but out of sight of land; and once a changada sailed from Pernambuco to Rio. Quainter, because more pretentious, were the barcaços. The small ones had the appearance, if not the actuality, of being dug-outs. Across their gunwales two beams are fastened, and under these and over the side, but touching and, I think, bolted to the gunwales, great logs of the very buoyant wood, used also for the changadas, almost as light as cork, as a sort of outrigger to keep them from capsizing. They have triangular sails with very long booms on very long whippy masts, as have the changadas. The larger barcaços, of 20 to 40 tons, are very obviously built rather than dug out. The wood used for planking is very intractable and is pieced together in short lengths; the wide seams are payed with a white lime stopping, so that the hull looks more than anything like a roughly built wall of dark red stone. And it is the shape of a wall too; in design it is not a great improvement on the dug-out. This wood is so hard that it is worm-proof; the boats are not painted at all below the water but kept scrubbed clean. They are rigged with two or three masts, occasionally with primitive shrouds, but in the main standing by their own stiffness, which is slight, though the heavy elastic wood is almost unbreakable. The foremast is a ridiculous little thing stuck right in the eyes of her, and the sail a substitute for jibs, of which they have none; it has a long boom which has to be topped up nearly to the foremast head to clear it over in stays. What surprised the crews of these vessels about our expedition was the small number of hands in so big a ship. They would expect half a dozen at the least. Which might be possible in the Tropics, where everyone can live on deck; but I find three is quite enough to house and feed.

A plumber was brought off to make a connexion from the forward fresh-water tank to the pantry pump, so that we could shift that fifty gallons without the business of dipping it out by hand. Other people were brought to scrape and paint and varnish, and at last the full moon came round, and I succeeded in getting high and dry on the sandbank, propped up on legs. It was not the nicest job, for there was a wicked current over the bank which cut away the sand from under the vessel. However, I had tackles on the legs, and kept adjusting them according as they or her keel sank the faster. This time again I had a wonderful tide, and the four negroes who were at the job got on three coats of paint.

One ought not to go about the world indiscriminately without having one's ship copper-sheathed. The bare wood requires constant painting and causes constant anxiety about worms; and one is far more likely to get 4-foot tides than 10-foot tides in Pernambuco, or indeed in any of what I may call oceanic ports, and docks and slipways are limited in number and particularly in distribution. The condition of my boat's bottom was a continual anxiety to me, though I was only once badly handicapped by weeds and not attacked at all by worms.

The evening tide was up to sample, and I floated off all right and went back to the anchorage to take stores on board. For so short a time I did not want to bother with my best bower and I lay on my second, a lighter, but a magnificently holding anchor, with only a wire rope. During the night, alas! a dredger, for dredgers here work night as well as day, got her mooring chains across my wire and ran down or carried away my anchor buoy. I hove up cautiously, but the lightest strain parted the wire; and that was the end of that anchor, except the compensation I got for it. Having thus lightened the ship by about a hundredweight forward, I took out some ballast aft to trim her. I think I took out about a ton. We really were too deep; that, I am sure, is why we got wetter in the North-East Trade than elsewhere.

The principal stores which we shipped were salt pork

in a barrel and dried beef in strips. Hitherto all our meat had been in tins, as we did not want to do unnecessary cooking in the hot weather; and after a straight diet of tins one has a craving for something solid to bite on. We laid in also rockets, to fire as we sailed out; I had previously bought a Brazilian flag to fly on that and other occasions. I bought it from a tailor, and as the tailor could only speak Portuguese we were interpreted by an Italian who described himself as "chronometrista" and occupied part of the tailor's shop. When the chronometrista heard that I was likely to return to Pernambuco he asked me to bring him a pair of rattle-snakes, and on my promising to do so set my barometer in order. But most of the shops only sell ordinary things, as ours do at home. I had acquired, somehow or another, a cricket, which, in default of a hearth, inhabited the coal bunker and piped a very familiar and homelike note. He did not survive long; I have no luck with live stock, but I gravely suspect my cook of having killed him under the impression that he was a cockroach. As if a well-conducted yacht would have cockroaches on board!

In spite of the delays I had enjoyed myself very much in Pernambuco. The town is fascinating. I believe most Portuguese towns are, but this one is a Dutch hybrid, and so much the more interesting. The right way to see strange ports is in one's own ship. One says, "We'll just slip across and have a look at South America." You can't do that in a mail steamer. And a mail steamer is rather foreign all the time, whereas we step straight out of that part of the Irish Free State which is the yacht *Saoirse* into the United States of Brazil. Here I had got into an atmosphere which the yachtsman who stays at home rarely enjoys. In some way he is cut off from other users of the sea. The professional mariner looks up to him if he is enormously rich, and down on him if he is not; and his amateurishness, sedulously cultivated to ensure his amateur status, forbids intercourse. But in a foreign port he has to do as other ship-masters do, and so becomes one of them, and a person of some consideration; he is given his courtesy rank, and a seat in the Captains' room at the ship-chandler's office. Here it was acknowledged that I was on a *bona-fide* foreign voyage; and I got my stores duty free, a privilege denied me in Dublin. It seemed the most natural thing to be travelling about the world in command of a vessel. It did not seem quite so natural to the port and police authorities, however; they insisted on my having some undisclosed motive, and eventually wrote me down as a surveying ship commissioned by the Admiralty, or something of that sort. At any rate they gave me a great send-off, even if they did charge me £5 for Light Dues.

I now had to take my voyage seriously. I had already said that just before we reached the Doldrums; but in fact I imagine reasonable care will always bring any reasonable yacht through that region as well as through the Trade Winds. When, eighteen months later, I was again at Pernambuco, I said quite sincerely, "I have finished sailing round the world; now I am going yachting towards Dublin." And, though an unknown bit of the South Atlantic lay before me, I said equally sincerely when Cape Horn came between me and the sunset, "Thank God I'm in home waters again." Not until one has run down one's easting round the three stormy capes does one realize that it is always a matter of concern. The hurricanes of the Tropics and the terrific storms of the North Atlantic have their seasons;

down South strong winds and high seas are usual, and she must be a stout vessel, well manned and in good trim, that does not sooner or later have to heave-to. Do not think I claim all this for my ship or for myself; I had an experience of light weather which was probably unique; but I never knew that there would not be a gale next day, and on the only occasion when it did blow hard there was a stupendous sea. In a fortnight or so I should be learning all about it. Meanwhile with a light breeze from a point or so north of east we were drawing off the land on a glassy sea; so the bugbear of the South-East Trade need hold no terrors.

For some reason, in spite of ideal weather and a clean bottom, we made indifferent progress. I discount the immediate start. I was sea-sick, P. had bad neuralgia, and H. thought to set up the topmast stay and it came away in his hand. But no one could remain sick long in these conditions. This was not that rude and cloudy Trade Wind which had chased us, drenched and staggered by steep cross-seas, down the uneasy North Atlantic; if we had a complaint it was that the wind was too light. This was a better sun that passed day by day over the sky which brought up only a few small tongues of crimson and orange flame against the sunset, and a bar or two of purple to divide the sunrise from the waning moon, but by day or by night was cloudless. The Devil whispers that now is the time when I should have an engine. Not so, friend Satan; I do not want to go any more to windward; I can sail some $4\frac{1}{2}$ knots, but in these light airs I could not sail at all if I had to drag a dead propeller; and where could I carry the oil that would run the engine for a thousand miles? A motor is no substitute for a topsail. Give me a bigger topsail.

73

While we were in these light Trades all hands slept all night, and all hands worked all day, P. most virtuously, overhauling and drying out the stores; H. and myself principally with our pens. However, for the sake of the ship I rigged an electric bell so that the helmsman could call the watch below without leaving the wheel, and I cut an opening from the chart-room to the galley, so that he could get his cocoa more safely than by carrying it across the deck; while H. made a weather-cloth for the poop rail. But we were mightily relieved when, on the evening of the ninth day, we saw a little group of clouds, differing slightly from the other clouds that drift across the Trade Wind area, hanging stationary above the horizon on our lee bow; for under them lay the island of Trinidada, and south of Trinidada we might expect a change, for better or for worse, in the weather.

Here was an island which had been seldom visited, and only once, in any sense, explored; here was a sea so smooth that the usually difficult landing would have been almost perfectly safe; and there is that word "almost" which deterred me from attempting it in a small canvas boat through water swarming with sharks, and hundreds of miles from any help. This is the one serious drawback to cruising in a very small yacht, that one cannot explore the more remote places of the world for want of sufficient boats and men to handle them. In case of accident to the landing party, I should have had to sail 600 miles to Bahia to borrow a boat, for I could hardly have risked the yacht within swimming distance, without a powerful motor to pull her out of trouble if she got into it; and by the time I got back from Bahia it is probable that the party would have died

74

either from eating land-crabs or from being eaten by them. One wants two good boats and five good men to make a job of it; one cannot take risks in mid-ocean. Observe my procedure that night.

I was steering for the channel between Trinidada and Martin Vaz. Now at sunset I had only seen the land-clouds over the former, being, as I judged, about 40 miles away. The latter, being low, I had not seen at all. It was an abominably dark night, I could see no horizon, and I only imagined that I could see a blacker patch of darkness to leeward than elsewhere. At midnight the islands should be abeam, for I had been cracking on in a moderate breeze of wind the better to ensure that no unsuspected current should set me out of my course. Was I carrying too much canvas? Was I risking getting dismasted somewhere near a lee shore which I could not see? Or was I giving that shore an excessive berth, to pile up on the low islets that lie on the windward side of the channel? At last I saw a little spot of blackness for an instant on the weather beam; that was Martin Vaz, and it might have been five miles away or it might have been one. I went through that channel like a scared cat, with all the deep-water man's panic upon me; and, note, that channel is 26 miles wide, and I was in a small and handy fore-and-after. Thus does the ocean make a coward of one.

At sunrise the fantastic peaks of Trinidada stood out for a few minutes, clear of their customary clouds, now far astern of us. There is a singular romance about these tiny outposts of earth pushed a thousand miles into the waters, barren masses of volcanic rock, once milestones on the long colonial passage, but now rarely seen by human eye: Penhedo de São Pedro, Ilha da Santissima

75

Trinidada, Tristan da Cunha, Amsterdam. We missed the first; here was the second, and our next objective was the third.

If another indication than Trinidada were wanting to show that we were approaching a fresh stage of our journey, we saw for the first time on the same day an albatross, which I qualify in my log-book by the words "as is supposed." In those days I must have been very sceptical about strange beasts, for he was as certainly *Diomedea Exulans* as he was a winged fowl, but I was badly provided with books and was under the impression that albatrosses only inhabited very far southern waters; whereas in fact they may be seen even North of the Equator, and rarely go beyond the 60th parallel. I think, however much one may have read about a thing, it comes as rather a shock when one actually sees it for the first time. I had read about albatrosses and penguins and icebergs, but in a stupid way, without really visualizing them, because I did not really believe in them; as people read who hold a book before them because they cannot sit still without something in their hands; or perhaps I should rather say, cannot meditate without appearing ridiculous. These things were not real to me because my northern-hemispherical mind could not project itself across the Equator; but now that it has followed my body to their habitat they are as real in the pages of a book as in the Southern Ocean. So I say the time to read books of travel is the present or the future; when one can keep up with the author he is a good companion on the road; when one swaps yarns with him on one's return he is still better; but no one that has never left this side can be intimate with a man who is stravaging round the other side of the world.

Many years ago I read Professor Moseley's *Challenger* book, and though I had a pretty catholic taste in Natural History and Moseley a delightful style, I did not appreciate it; recently I picked it up, to verify an opinion, and did not put it down till long past midnight. If, therefore, gentle reader, you do not understand this book of mine, put it from you, sail round the world, and perhaps when you come back you will know what I mean.

On the following day we lost the Trades in lat. 22° S., and very soon our surroundings began to change. The increase in bird life was most conspicuous. The avifauna of the Tropics is very poor; a few Bosun birds and a solitary gannet who had probably strayed north on a fishing excursion from Trinidada were all I noticed; but now albatrosses were seen by twos and threes, and Cape pigeons by scores. We had seen the last of the flying-fish, but bonitos and dolphins were still with us, feeding, I suppose, on something else which I did not see and could not catch; their beat was shared by an occasional whale and innumerable porpoises; all in increasing numbers as we drew to the southward.

We went slowly enough at first, as the winds were still very light, though what there was came from the northeast, and the sea stayed always smooth; we sent up the foreyard and bent and set the sail, and went a little faster; on the third day we were making over 6 knots with a moderate breeze, still from the same quarter; on the fifth, in lat. 30° S. and long. 20° W., the Devil tempted me and I fell. He can put a very specious appearance on his temptations; the wind had gone more northerly, there was a considerable swell, and admittedly we were running to the eastward of our proper

77

course; and on that 16th day of September there was
no harm done. Only on the following day I should have
made more southing, even at the cost of taking in all
the fore-and-aft canvas. The tempter hinted that as we
were so near Table Bay (1,750 miles, to be precise), 150
miles a day in that direction were better than 100 in any
other; that what we wanted was gentle northerly
breezes and not westerly gales; that we had lit the galley
stove for the first time that day on the verge of the
Tropics, and what should we feel like any farther
south? and, lastly, that if we went too near to Tristan
da Cunha the inhabitants would come out and massacre us for omitting to bring their mail. So next day
we found that we had so much more easting than southing that we had to hypothecate a strong current to
account for our position; when the Devil puts his hand
to a job he does it thoroughly. And even the day after
we were sailing so fast and easily that I let her go on the
same course. When at last I woke up to the fact that I
had not yet reached the 33rd parallel and was actually
getting set to the northward of east, it was too late to
remedy my mistake, as it was blowing up for a southerly
gale, with a rising sea. By the evening of the 20th of
September we had sent down the foreyard and put two
reefs in the mainsail, and were reaching along fairly
comfortably, though slowly enough.

The earlier part of this day was splendid sailing.
There was a big swell coming down from the North,
the relic of the good breezes of the past two days, and a
big and increasing sea running up from the South, but
not so much wind behind it as to make it dangerously
steep or breaking. With these opposing sets of waves
there was no oscillatory movement of the water; the

ship merely rose and fell, 20 feet at a time, going along as steady as a racing yacht in the Solent, with the foam just lapping the lee covering-board. There is no pleasanter sensation than sailing along a really big beam sea, but it is one in which one can seldom indulge, and only for a short time. Soon we had to reduce sail, and haul our wind so as to take the seas on the bow; for by now the old swell was nearly extinguished and the new one was running into steep breaking crests. Next morning it was blowing a gale, right ahead on our course; I had taken in jib and mizzen, and we were head-reaching under staysail and mainsail, both close-reefed. Neither the wind nor the sea was worse than what one expects off our own coasts; the nuisance was that it was a foul wind. A foul wind in the open ocean is, however, generally a remediable nuisance, so I gave up sailing very slowly in a considerably wrong direction, and went off at large to look for a fair wind.

Before embarking on the next paragraph, in which I shall have to use some words of strange meaning, I must explain that there is no term in the English language that denotes unequivocally a system of winds rotating round an area of low pressure. The depression beloved of the weather forecaster does not quite fill the bill; besides, it is ambiguous to say "The depression has passed away from us." So I fall back, as the meteorologist does, on "cyclone" for the whole system, and, for brevity, "storm centre" for the middle of it, without implying any particular strength of wind. For this purpose I use the word "gale" suitably qualified. Thus "half a gale" means a wind blowing up to 30 miles an hour; a "gale" to 40; a "fresh gale", "whole gale," "strong gale" may approach 50, but is generally a simple "gale" complicated by cold rain or a catastrophe in the galley.

It was obvious that the storm centre was somewhere to the northward; it was probable that it was moving to the eastward; but I had no indication of how far away it lay, and the barometer was very sluggish and unhelpful. But if I kept the ship running before the wind I should eventually get a westerly breeze, and I supposed the barometer would tell me if I were getting imprudently near the centre. It did not; this depression was, like most extra-tropical cyclones, a saucer-shaped affair; and as we proceeded to the northward the wind actually took off a little. In the evening the dull and rather thick weather cleared, and I saw a great commotion in the upper clouds and deduced that we were pretty near the centre. The whole affair must have been quite stationary, or even moving in the wrong direction. While the wind was still tolerably steady we hove-to and had dinner, and then waited to see what would happen.

It fell a calm, then the waves, no longer controlled by any order, ran in every direction, climbed upon each other's backs, and hurled misshapen lumps of black water into the air; at times it felt as if they were hurling the ship into the air as well. We had a good view of all this, for right above our heads the moon hung in a small clear space of sky. Round her black clouds, throwing out here and there streamers of brilliant white, whirled in a mad dance, at one moment retreating almost to the horizon which was lurid with lightning, at another rushing towards the charmed centre. At last one invaded it, and there burst into rain. It was overwhelming, stunning. I at the wheel could not see the compass a foot away. The mate, from the shelter of the chart-room, bawled out instructions to me, for I wanted to get steerage way on the ship as soon as possible. Though the wind had eased off gradually, it might come on again with a bang and knock the mast out of us. I do not know just when the wind did come; very little of it was enough to give me command of the ship, for that deluge had knocked the sea flat; and it came gradually, with intervals of calm and comparatively light showers. It was not the conventional behaviour of a cyclone, but since the dirt started the barometer had only dropped fifteen-hundredths of an inch.

Daybreak saw us running before a fresh westerly breeze, and I set the jib and turned one reef out of the mainsail. I should have turned out the crew and sent up the foreyard, but I felt we all needed a bit of rest, and sending up that foreyard was likely to be an all-hands and all-the-morning job. We had not shipped any heavy seas, so it must have been the rain that washed all the gear into an inextricable tangle. By the time that things had dried out and been to some extent cleared up, there was far too much wind and sea to set the sail; for we had now got on the right side of the weather and into a smart westerly gale.

This was my first experience of easting weather. I had sworn, in these circumstances, to take in my mainsail and run under square canvas only. For to a small vessel sea is usually a more serious matter than wind, and if it is really big she has to steer dead before it, and chance a gybe. Being without a main boom we could take that chance, but naturally preferred a rig which eliminated all risk. To-day, however, since I could not set any square canvas, I wanted to avoid reducing the fore-and-afters, nuisance as they were in a heavy sea; for I was not wasting a fair wind. I let the ship run on under two headsails and single-reefed mainsail. I wanted to bring the wind as far out on the starboard quarter as I dared, to make up some of that southing I had lost the day before, and that kept all the sails full, so they were not so much of a nuisance as I had expected. But looking back on it, the sea was not so bad as I thought it was; the ship, however, took a lot of steering, and I took P.'s watch for him. Part of the difficulty of steering was due to the cramped position of the helmsman, but part was due to the benefactions of a friend in Dublin, who had insisted that the wheel chains were not strong enough, and had rove off a stouter chain. Meanwhile the unlucky P. had kicked the original chain overboard. The new chain, naturally enough, jammed in the sheaves when a strain came on it, and, such is the perversity of inanimate things, jammed worst at such moments as I, fearing the ship would broach to, wanted to put the helm hard up. With my heart in my mouth I had to let the wheel run back a spoke or two and have another try at it. I dared not force it for fear of breaking something. But all that evening we ran unscathed.

Dark mountain ranges, their lower slopes netted with the tracery of spindrift, reared snowy crests against the sky; from them jutted sharp-cut spurs, which, growing with incredible rapidity, exploded against the bulwarks and discharged a salvo of spray into the belly of the sails. The ship, her jib-boom sweeping the water already mottled by the fountain thrown from her cutwater, rose on the steep face of the advancing swell and drowned the lighter patter of the drops torn from its summits with the shrieking in the rigging of the now unimpeded wind; then with a great crash the sea spread out under her in a boiling sheet of white. On this, or, as it seemed, suspended over this, and uncontrolled by contact with the firm support of the waters, she flew for a long space, then gradually settled down on the streaked back of the roller; the singing of the wind in the stays dropped to a low murmur, and in an uncanny quiet she shook herself and prepared for the next onset. So hour after hour the rhythm goes on, a hissing, rattling, shrieking crash; and then the bubbling of foam; a hypnotic influence. H. said that I was asleep when he relieved me at the wheel, but I do not believe that was literally true.

I have very frequently been asked whether my sails, which on a day like this would be little more than twenty feet above the water level, were not becalmed between the seas. What I have described in the last paragraph certainly gave the illusion of being becalmed; but it was, I imagine, only an illusion, due to the facts that on the back of a wave one is undoubtedly moving slowly because one is sailing uphill, and that one is in smooth water after a very noisy and agitated few moments. It is physically impossible that the wind should be lighter on this, the windward, slope of the sea, where one might expect a calm would be close under the crest; but here, it seemed to me, probably because it was puffy, that it blew the hardest. In connexion with this I noticed one fact that surprised me very much, that there was always a smooth depression in the crest immediately astern of us (I was not using oil, it was just Providence) and one might expect a strong wind to blow over that as it would over a mountain pass. But the fact that I lost no sails running in heavy weather proves that the puffs cannot have been very heavy or the soft spots very light.

We had now managed to get back to lat. 32° S., but in long. 4° W. the wind left us again. Properly we should have been somewhere about the 40th parallel, though I learned afterwards that conditions had been abominable down there; anywhere between was full of easterly winds. But it was too late to try to get South now; I had to make the best of the latitude I was in.

As a matter of fact I made a poor use of one fine day, on which I logged a very light westerly breeze and a confused swell. I had all the fore-and-afters in and drifted along under foresail only, while all the clothes and bedding, books and potatoes were hauled up on deck. We seem to have indulged in this amusement far more often in the early stages of the voyage than later, much to the detriment of our sailing record; whether because the decks were more leaky then, or because we were still struggling with the awful legacy of that first three weeks' culture of mildews I do not know. Even crossing the Indian Ocean, with a crew none of whom was conspicuous for the domestic virtues, though the ship was indescribably filthy it was with inoffensive filth; and of course after I had shipped a Tongan crew everything was beautifully clean. At this stage, however, there was mighty little result to show for our labours, except an unnecessarily slow passage. To be quite just, though, I ought not to forget that the wind was right aft, very light, and with a confused swell; as happened at times also in the Indian and Pacific Oceans, where, too, the fore-and-afters had occasionally to be taken in;

but then I had half as much square canvas again, the foretopsails, and those so light that an air would fill them. As things were, I had soon to put the potatoes back in their locker, the books in the shelves, the bedding on the bunks, and the clothes on my back (for it was getting cold and windy) and turn my attention to dealing with the weather according to the rules of Storm Sailing; which meant a hopeful attempt to keep the ship in that quadrant of the approaching cyclone which provided a fair wind for Table Bay.

Now while it is generally true of the South Atlantic that the winds are easterly in the Tropics, northerly off Brazil, westerly to the southward, and southerly up the African Coast, there are modifications in detail. Nowhere can one be sure of a westerly wind; even in 55° S. I have met a North-Easter. One does not run down one's easting with the wind all the time right aft, but with it anywhere from north to south-west; the rapidity of its changes depending on the distance of the ship from the centres of the depressions, and their relative speeds. I had located one depression to the southward, unpleasantly near, and moving irregularly; which meant shifty winds and a consequently cross-sea. These things generally travel in company; all I could do was to stay where I was and hope that the next one that came along would move with the same speed and in the same direction as myself. If it travelled, as it properly should, towards Cape Agulhas at 7 knots, we should be in Table Bay in three days. But wherever it went I was determined to keep to the northward of it, and chance head winds and a foul current later on. It started nicely on the 28th of September with a moderate north-west gale, for which we were ready, stripped to jib and foresail.

85

This day I noticed quite unprecedented swarms of birds: albatrosses, mollymawks, giant petrel, Cape pigeons, Mother Carey's chickens, and most profusely, prions. It is said that a profusion of these in the middle latitudes indicates severe weather farther south. If so, I was well off where I was; the weather just suited me, and I did not want it any more severe. This time we were running dead before the sea and could admire its majesty without being terrified by its steepness; all of us except the helmsman, that is; for there is a law of the Medes and Persians that he may not look behind him. So long as he kept the ship straight she steered so easily that broaching-to was unthinkable; but if he saw those blue cliffs rolling up astern he might lose his head, and our lives. By way of encouragement to P., I slept under his hand, so to say, in the chart-room during his watch; not perhaps the wisest thing in the world, for if we got pooped, and one must always remember the possibility of the most unlikely accident, the chart-room would certainly be filled up and I should probably be drowned. For there was a big sea that night. I have seen bigger off Eagle Island in Mayo, and off Cape Leeuwin in Australia, but only one of each; there were eight hours of these. There is, however, something about my yacht, probably her very clean run, that tames the ugliest-looking following sea, and we did not take a drop of water on deck, except of course in the way of that unlucky galley skylight.

Of all the outward passage the thing that sticks most firmly in my memory is next morning's sunrise. We were, as usual, off our course, for the sun was right ahead when he was a full span above the horizon, which was piled with the cast-off clouds of last night's gale; so

for the most part, to me at the wheel, he was hidden behind the foresail, and his glare did not blind me to
subtler colourings. And this is what I saw. First, because
it was nearest, and because I was rather anxious as to
whether it would blow away, the great square of the
foresail, with a warm brownish light filtering through
the wet canvas; across it slashed the broad purple
shadow of the jib, and the harder tracery of stays and
spilling-lines. Then, under the high arch of its foot, water
with the unreflecting blackness of pitch, but where it
was drawn up by the gale into narrow ridges against the
level rays of light showing near at hand a transparency
from deep emerald to palest aquamarine, and farther
off a mere greenish fluorescence over the dead blackness,
till at the horizon the two tints blending together passed
out of sight beneath a luminous lemon haze that separ-
ated the dark water from the dark bank of cloud. And
this luminous haze came back from the dawn towards
the ship, and then one realized that it was but spindrift,
spread like a gossamer veil over the whole ocean, but by
some trick of the steepness of the sea or of the incidence
of the light alone showing that path towards the sun
which commonly rests upon the waters.

I have said we were off our course; that in itself is
nothing, if we can be as much off it on the other side to-
morrow; it is the normal thing for so small a vessel. For
when it blows from the north we may have to run somewhat to the southward of our course to ease the ship;
when it blows from the westward we still run to the
southward to bring the old sea right aft; and when it
blows from the southward it blows hard, and we quite
certainly have to run to the northward to disarm the
tempest. So, on the whole, we ought to find it easier to

make southing; but not here and now. The storm on which we were riding was not doing the right thing. It was moving to the northward of east, and passing out ahead of us. The wind and sea now having moderated, I tried to keep in the southerly sector. It was no good; the wind backed continuously towards the south-east and the sea got up again. It is, I repeat, generally true that the wind blows this way up the African coast. And there was a strong current setting with the wind, and a very short way to leeward the South-East Trade; and if I avoided all these and managed to struggle down the coast, before I reached Table Bay I should probably meet the wind that really does blow, the Curse of the Cape, the South-Easter; for it was the season. With many groans I got on the other tack and sailed back in the direction of Tristan da Cunha, to wait for a slant, or at least for an intermission of the fiendish sea which reduced me to four knots and three points of leeway; or thereabouts. I will not dogmatize about these figures. Before this I had said in my pride that at any moment I could give the ship's position within 5 miles. This scotched another bugbear; I had been assured that in so small a boat astronomical observations would be quite untrustworthy. But I remember a stormy scene with my navigator in the times when we had a sweep on the day's run; he maintaining it was 165·6, which would give it to the higher draw, and I insisting on 165·4. And the day when he swore that the sun was North of us, and I swore it was South; and we both found its altitude to be 90 degrees no minutes or seconds. But on that day there was a fine big swell, which raised, it is supposed, the axis of the telescopes in our sextants 20 feet above mean sea-level just when the sun passed over our meridian; now there was no swell; we stood just 10 feet above the water and the waves stood all round obscuring half the sky; our navigation was the merest guesswork.

Fortunately it was not always like this. There was that very calm day when three albatrosses swam round the ship, and H. told me off to feed them with bread and jam by hand while he stood by with his camera; they were afraid of food-stuffs unwontedly suspended in mid-air, and I was very much more afraid of their beaks, so the result was not entirely a success. There was that lovely day when P. actually caught a bonito, somewhat marred by the fact that he put half the carcase into the harness cask, and the result of that was disastrous. Our navigation was rather more successful. We did eventually get a slant of wind, but it did not take us all the way into Table Bay, but left us lying on a calm hot afternoon on a smooth and peaceful sea, just within sight of a hazy hill-top which might have been the Dassenberg. Suddenly we were startled by a rumbling noise. It could hardly be thunder; it sounded more like big guns. Could another war have broken out? Our news was nearly five weeks old. In readiness to take advantage of the provisions of Article 48 of our Constitution I hoisted the ensign of the Irish Free State and pinned such of the ship's papers as had any reference to Great Britain carefully behind those that bore the words "Saorstat Eireann." At last two small steam vessels appeared through the haze; if they were patrol trawlers it was not their guns I heard, but heavier metal. Then something broke water quite near us. Heavens! a submarine; and what we heard was the explosion of torpedoes. And then H., from half-way up the rigging, sang out "Ah bloooow!" We had run into a pod of humpback whales and the supposed warships were massacring them with harpoon guns, a very noisy instrument. I did not see the operations close to; no great loss. Later I was to see them from a whaler's gun platform.

Meanwhile we were 60 miles from Table Bay, and becalmed. The coal-bunker was swept clean—Lord! what a coal-eater was that galley stove; but we had kept it going day and night since it was lit. That did not worry me, for the weather now was summery, not to say sultry. The salt pork was all spoiled by that confounded bonito. That did worry me, because it is such a lubberly thing to put a bonito into a harness cask, especially when I had given strict orders against it. We drifted to the southward somehow during the night and at nine o'clock of the morning of the 6th of October— eight days for what I hoped to do in three—saw more land; this time the right land, the colossal wall of Table Mountain and the Twelve Apostles rising above the haze. Here we were greeted by a steam trawler, who had recognized us from the "pictures" in Cape Town that week. I had originally given the 1st of October as my date of arrival; but after I had wasted so much time in Brazil the experts said I should not get there till the 20th. Naturally there is some uncertainty about the arrival of a sailing vessel, but there need not be all that much. I measure the Great Circle distance, divide by 100 and call it days; that is near enough to calculate one's stores on.

I was going to get a new mast and a thorough refit in Cape Town, so when a breeze of wind came along, a fine, slashing south-westerly breeze, with no sea under it, I did not shorten sail for it. At first for the sake of

appearances; this was a Saturday, a day peculiarly con-
secrated to yachting, and if the Table Bay yachtsmen
were expecting me I wanted to make my entry in style.
Then I saw the cloth being laid on Table Mountain,
and had to carry on before the South-Easter struck me;
if I could make my number before I was dismasted, some
one would come out and tow me in. Lastly, we had all
got into shoregoing clothes, and could not afford to
pick up sails from a deck which was knee-deep in water.
Everything held out, though I dared not look at the
mast-head; but I was not going to start the gaff-
topsail sheet till I was in the lee of the mountains. Then
the yacht hove herself up, poured the water through the
ports and shook her sails at the impending cliffs, and
when I saw the harbour launch making towards us I
think we stripped off those sails in record time.

Was this, you ask, cutting a dash in Table Bay? Yes,
on the whole, it was. Coasting yachts may like to sail
into harbour, but deep-water ships expect to be towed
to their berth when they come in from a passage across
the ocean.

CHAPTER IV

A SOUTH AFRICAN INTERLUDE

When I left Pernambuco I had some intention of saving the three weeks I had lost there by leaving out my proposed call at Table Bay and making a direct run to Australia. But in spite of the fact that the local Press had announced this as being my very firm intention and had added that I should do the run in 25 days *"seguramente,"* whatever that means, for I am no Portuguese scholar, before I was half-way across the Atlantic I realized that it was a very foolish intention and that its fulfilment would probably take me more than three times as long. When I got a little farther the state of the winds made it quite certain that I could only get direct to Australia by going overland across Africa; and before I reached Africa a number of small repairs and alterations which required workshop facilities became desirable though not urgently necessary. It was not until I knew I was going into harbour and would start the refit in two days that I began breaking things up. That mast was not any more use, the mizzen gooseneck was all crumpled up and only a miracle kept the boom in its place; the jib-stay was stranded and was slack enough anyway, for the jib-boom had crushed the fid so badly that it had come in an inch or two; and the sheave of the main halliard block had broken to pieces and fallen out, and a fractured edge had damaged the wire.

A SOUTH AFRICAN INTERLUDE

I do not want anyone to suppose that this is the sort of condition in which I make passages over the oceans; in all probability everything, except the mizzen gooseneck, which I could have replaced with jaws, would have held out to Australia, but that race with the South-Easter into Table Bay was a splendid opportunity of testing to destruction everything that ought to be destroyed. All the way down the Atlantic I had been thinking of better ways of rigging my rather experimental gear, and I had always intended to spend a fortnight over this refit.

The mainmast embodied the worst mistake in the ship, a mistake which seems to me extremely common among yachts and the like with pole masts. It was a very nice-looking piece of larch, but the tree was rather too light, and though it was strong enough up to the hounds, it tapered evenly from there to the topmast head. Consequently if one were indiscreet in the use of flying kites one would not lose a topmast only, but might lose a considerable part of the lower mast. As a matter of fact it is more likely to go somewhere in the masthead, for that is generally the worst stayed part of the spar and has the suddenest and most unfair strains put upon it. I do not say that my system of staying is ideal, but I did not alter it; indeed I could not without compromising the foresail, which on a voyage like this is really the most important sail in the ship; I am, however, perhaps unduly heavy on head-stays; I scrapped two topmast stays and two jib-stays. It seems rather remarkable that the much lighter backstays, which one would have thought had more work to do, stood all right, until one realizes that in the matter of strain a fresh breeze to a vessel close-hauled is worse than a fresh gale to a vessel running. I had more confidence in the new mast, a stick of Oregon pine, for it was properly nicked, and if the topmast went over the side nothing else would follow it; and I also had confidence that the backstays would keep it from going over the side, and my flying-jib, from being a piece of braggadocio, became a habit.

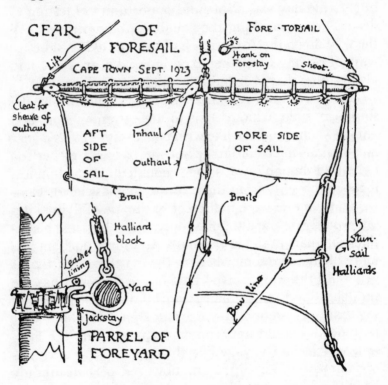

GEAR OF FORESAIL

CAPE TOWN SEPT. 1923

FORE · TOPSAIL

Lift

Hank on Forestay

Shoot

Cleat for sheave of outhaul

AFT SIDE OF SAIL

Inhaul

Outhaul

FORE SIDE OF SAIL

Brail

Brails

Halliard block

Leather lining

Yard

Jackstay

PARREL OF FOREYARD

Stun-sail Halliards

Bow line

The gear of the foresail naturally called for improvement, now that I had learned the conditions under which it would be used—namely, with the widest possible range of winds; and, when they became impossibly scant, furled as snugly as we could manage without sending the yard down on deck. Still, as we sometimes had to lower the yard, I had a parrel made which was jammed so tightly by the downward pull of the chain jackstay against the halliards that it held the yard to the mast at any height with comparatively little play and consequent wear.

To extend the use of the foresail as far as possible I fitted catheads for the tacks, and bowlines leading to the jib-boom end; they were a vanity, for on a wind they could not be used along with the mainsail, which was generally of more value at such times. Then the foresail had to be got out of the way. It could not well be furled by hand, as one would have to stand in the rigging to pass the gaskets; but the two brails, rigged as sketched on the preceding page, did it adequately. Only the fact that their falls came down forward of the sail made the operation dangerous at times; I have since led them through bull's-eyes worked in the centre seam of the sail, so that the hauling part is abaft all. Now, also, I have fixed a strong becket to the bottom of the seam, by which it can be bowsed down taut, and each half of the sail furled independently; which is, as near as may be, an ideal rig.

Since my square canvas was patently inadequate, I had two triangular topsails, or raffees, made of aeroplane linen, which proved invaluable on the rest of the voyage, and so nearly fool-proof that they were used even off the Horn.

Here I made considerable purchases of small chain, and spliced a fathom or two into my running gear wherever there was a short nip. A chain splice is a queer thing; you take two strands only, demoralize them thoroughly by hauling them through and bending them over a very small link; and then find the splice is the strongest part of the rope. And the moral of that is that one gains strength by leaning up against something stronger than one's self. It is a commonplace that a small sailing yacht is stronger than her crew, but it is no harm to make her many times stronger, so that her excess of strength may irradiate her surroundings. Having originally made my yacht's hull as strong as possible, the only excess of virtue available was watertightness; to which end I put pipes to drain the cockpit into the sea. I was quite tired with pumping out of the bilges all the rain that fell on the night of the 21st of September. Besides, some day a sea might come on board, though in fact it never did.

I gave the necessary orders that these things should be done, and we took our three selves and the chronometer to live ashore while the vessel was handed over to the dockyard.

We were all three put up at the same Club, as was almost inevitable, seeing that we had arrived in the guise of three yachtsmen, partners in the enterprise; but it was a mistake. I should have gone elsewhere, for it is not wise for a captain to live with his crew lest they should presume on his familiarity.

It was a thousand pities that I saw Cape Town immediately after Pernambuco, for Cape Town is by no means the second most beautiful city in the world. Had I seen it after Melbourne or Auckland I should have appreciated thoroughly the really charming features of its older quarters as much as I did the really excellent architecture of the new houses in the suburbs; but I was overcome by the failure of the place as a city. The Huguenots and Dutch, whose tradition informs anything that is of any value, were not builders of towns;

the British Colonial is even less a builder of towns than
is his brother at home. The most he can hope to achieve
is a collection of tolerable houses; what he most frequently does achieve is a collection of intolerable
houses; and I do not suppose that Adderley Street is
very much better or worse than Regent Street will be.
But what a pitiful waste of opportunities! Excluding the
docks (though why docks should not have beautiful features I do not know, they have at Pernambuco and at
Auckland), there is a long length of waterfront backed by
mean sheds and public-houses; one cannot see a decent
building from the Bay. It is proposed some day to extend
the docks over part of this; I hope the day will come soon;
the ugliest tramp steamer is better than that desolation.

Even the most perverse efforts of man cannot spoil
the natural magnificence of Table Bay, nor the natural
beauty of its surroundings. I am temperamentally a stay-
at-home person, and I liked the Cape because it reminded me of home, or rather of the South of England;
it was settled and cultivated for one thing; for another
its woods of oak and pine were refreshing after man-
groves and palms. The road to Simondium might have
lain across a Dorset heath, but that instead of furze-
bushes there were 10-foot proteas with flowers the size
of cabbages; the town of Paarl might have been in the
Vale of Evesham, were it not for the stupendous
polished dome of the Paarl Rock and the fantastic ridge
of the Drakensberg. Paarl and Simondium were the only
places at any distance that I was able to visit; this was
an expedition by motor-car in which we were helping
the foreman shipwright to buy oak; and it was just the
oak woods that pleased me so much. We did not see a
great deal else, for we became rather deeply implicated

in the annual wine show which we ran into at Paarl. There was along with me another deep-sea yachtsman, the captain of a Danish boat built in China from Colin Archer's design, and on her way from Shanghai to Copenhagen. The local wine-growers wanted to give each of us a case of their best, and we of course had to sample a good deal to decide on what best suited our individual tastes. I am afraid it may be suggested that we sampled rather too thoroughly when I confess that when I opened my case—after getting to sea—I found it full of the horrid sweet stuff beloved of Scandinavians; and I suppose Captain I. was equally disgusted to be stuck with the dry types that I had selected. Apart from this, it was a most enjoyable day; one had all the amenities of our familiar landscape, with a lot of splendid mountains thrown in. Here one cannot get away from the mountains; except to seaward they bound every horizon, and especially near Cape Town, where they rise abruptly from a level plain, seem to justify any height with which the tricks of the atmosphere may happen to invest them.

I was not able to explore any of the outlying ranges, for they are not yet made accessible by roads and inns, and any ascent involves a considerable expedition; but I spent a good deal of time on Table Mountain, for if I intended to try Mount Cook two months hence I wanted all the climbing practice I could get. Any sort of sea-voyage is demoralizing to the pedestrian, but a voyage in a very small boat is disastrous to the mountaineer; for when one cannot walk without holding on to something, or stand unless with one foot jammed against the bulwarks and the other against the spare spars, one's sense of balance becomes atrophied, and one's legs do not instinctively plant themselves under one's centre of gravity, even on solid immovable rock. So I hoped that the climbers who were to show me the way up the mountain would come provided with ropes to haul me up the worst of the way; for the steep parts of Table Mountain are very steep. But the structure of the rock enables one to pass in comparative ease and safety over the most sensational crags, for though nominally a sandstone, under the influence of the weather it dissolves like limestone in holes and crannies apt for finger or toe, and faceted knobs growing out of the living rock and strong enough to swing a man's weight upon. By these means, and not without the safeguard of the rope, for I was not ashamed to admit that a five weeks' voyage had left me very wobbly about the knees, I got to the top of the cliff, which looks as smooth and straight as a wall from the town below, but from above is seen to be split by steep gullies and fronted by free-standing towers.

What a top that was! I looked over great sloping sheets of rock, fantastically grooved and tunnelled, down to the Southern Ocean; as, standing at Dun Ængus, I have looked over the bare blue slabs of Aran, down to Galway Bay; but with a difference. One can walk over the limestone of Aran, stepping across the narrow cracks in which lurk male-fern and maidenhair; the Table Mountain sandstone is split by chasms 10 feet wide and 30 feet deep, choked with giant heaths and proteas. But near by the elements have proved too strong for the rocks—the mountain is about the same height as Snowdon—and all has been washed away except some few isolated fragments, worn into the queerest shapes, that stand like Mesozoic monsters on the level surface of the subjacent slab.

On such levels, on any place where moisture can lodge, and especially on the wet ledges of the cliffs, grow the most varied flora in the world. Heaths of forty kinds, brooms, and proteas of a hundred different forms on the more exposed tops; then lilies, gladioli, and tall dog-daisies; on this wide shady shelf a sheet of arum lilies, and under the mossy dripping of that narrow gully the great red orchis, the Disa, pride of the Cape. All these Nature planted on the mountain; it was man that planted the woods, in some places, as it seems to me, especially as seen from below, too exclusively coniferous; but it was a Government scheme and therefore has an economic aspect. But beyond this sombre forest, where the spires of the spruce rise more sparsely through the pale mist of the silver-leaf and the thinner blue haze of the eucalyptus, and oaks and their congeners sweep down the rocky ravines and gradually merge into the gardens of Kirstenbosch (for all this side is a reserve for the protection of the native flora in which the rarer and more delicate plants are tended), there you will see woodlands as beautiful as any in the world. I know, for I have slept there. In this delightful climate the city man goes out in the evening and pitches his camp; at sunrise he crosses the mountain and is down in time to open his office at the appointed hour. So near is the town; when one sits on the edge of the Table one seems to be swinging one's legs over Oranjezicht.

This was the morning before a South-Easter; one of those hard clear mornings when there is no very definite light in the sky or anywhere else, merely a sort of yellowness between the dark bars of a cloud; but on the purple mountains every rock-face and gully showed up as clear as if picked out by the beam of some luminary

other than ours. From the Dassenberg to Cape Hang-
klip their serrated skyline ran in a great semicircle, at
the nearest some 30 miles away, to the north and to the
south rising beyond salt water, and in the middle beyond a plain no less level, and seeming even less substantial beneath a pale blue haze that veiled the crudity
of black pinewood and yellow sand.

I had also considerable distractions down at the docks.
Yacht cruising was being much talked of at the time;
besides the slightly larger Danish boat that had come in
three days before us another was expected from England. Consequently we had plenty of visitors with in-
vitations for lavish entertainments, and I regret to say
that we did not keep as sharp an eye as we should have
on the shipwrights. The one thing any fuss was made
about would have been better left alone; sundry critics
condemned the new mast, which was unnecessary,
though it was not quite up to yachting standard, and
talked about getting another one in the hearing of the
foreman, which was imprudent. He got that mast
stepped in record time when no one was looking, the
results of which I was to discover later. I find that the
methods of refitting a patrol yacht in Greenock and a
cruising yacht in Cape Town are the same; nothing is
done for ten days, and for four so many men are getting
in each other's way that the unfortunate mate cannot
see what is or what is not being done.

I had meant to spend a fortnight in Table Bay, but it
was the third Sunday after our arrival, October the
28th, when we drove down from the Club in two han-
som cabs—singular in being the only one-horse vehicles
at the Cape—and found all Cape Town there to see us
off, and also the Danish yacht *Shanghai*, that was sailing

that day for Copenhagen. We could not sail out of the docks, for there was no wind at all, but we had two offers of a tow, and two Government tugs, without saying anything, were standing by in case we wanted help. The other good Samaritans were, firstly, one of His Majesty's light cruisers, going to Simon's Bay. I hated to refuse a 50-mile free tow, but I knew the Navy too well. They would be sure to carry something away, as an excuse for taking us on into Simon's Bay; and the hospitality of the Royal Navy is worse than that of the Royal Cape Yacht Club when one is already a week behind one's time. Secondly, the *Shanghai*, which was providentially fitted with an engine. I gave the Captain some charts of the North Atlantic Islands, which I supposed I should not want again, but of course I do, for what yacht owner could refrain from revisiting Madeira and the Canaries? and he gave me some coast sheets of South Africa, which at first I refused with scorn, having no further interest in that continent, but which I found very useful later on.

So we towed out of harbour through a dense crowd of vessels of every kind, for the Yacht Club and the Railways and Harbours Administration vied with each other in obstructing our progress; and out in the bay a little air of wind came along and the *Shanghai* went off to the northward, it was presumed towards St. Helena; and we to the southward, it was presumed towards Lyttelton.

With a little breeze next morning and great help from the new foretopsails I managed to take my departure from Cape Point by noon; and after that was more calm, while we drifted at large over the Agulhas Bank, but always making something to the southward. Then, the foresail hanging up and down the mast, I noticed that

the forestay was all in a bight. I had told those shipwrights to put the fittings on the new mast exactly as
they had been on the old one, and in particular how to
secure this forestay. After three days of calm, it had
come down 3 inches. I wedged it up and made it taut
and safe, and then looked round for other defects.

No. 2. The fore-halliards were only seized on to the
collar of the forestay, instead of being on a strop round
the masthead; no wonder the stay came down.

No. 3. The step of the mast was cut wrongly and the
mast had not the same rake as the old one, which spoiled
her steering.

No. 4. In stepping the new mast the forward fresh-
water supply pipe had been broken. The culprits neither
did nor said anything, but hid the break under the floor.
Consequence, a third of my fresh water ran into the
bilges.

No. 5. Two main shrouds had half a turn in them, so
that the Matthew Walker came in a rounded hole in the
deadeye, and the last turn of the lanyard over a sharp
edge. One of them was stranded.

No. 6. The parrel of the foreyard, which was made in
two halves bolted together, was too small. They just
put in longer bolts, with no washers or anything to heave
the nuts up tight against, so naturally they dropped out.
I burred the threads over with a hammer and hoped they
would not drop out again before I had washers made.
They did. I cannot imagine why I cut up and drilled
holes in iron plates instead of hard wood; I suppose I
thought, "A washer is a washer; it is a piece of iron with
a hole in the middle."

No. 7. The new mizzen gooseneck was so designed
that it was not safe to use the sail in a fresh breeze.

No. 8 was discovered next day. There was a fresh breeze and the steering gear jammed. The chains, which were disconnected to let the carpenters get at the floor of the cockpit, had been rove off with a cross in them. It would not have been much trouble to reeve them off correctly in harbour, but it was a nasty messy job in a rough sea. This might have been a good opportunity for sea-anchor drill—which as a matter of fact we never had, for the thing was not used at all—but there were so many other things to do that it was a great relief to me to find that the ship would run quite straight under jib only and with the rudder wedged amidships.

No. 9 was the ship-chandler's affair, not the ship-wright's. I had ordered, and paid for, American salt beef, which is the only sort one can depend on in that part of the world. What they gave me had to be thrown overboard this day.

I admit that I was very much to blame for not looking after the work; but it was not just for the mate and steward to throw stones, for they had each told me categorically to go away and play and not interfere with their business. They were inclined to pooh-pooh the whole affair, and suggested that we might call at Amsterdam Island for water and beef. This made me wild. Even if I could find Amsterdam Island, imagine two very indifferent boatmen going in a 10-foot canvas dinghy to a notoriously bad landing-place on an uninhabited island 2,000 miles from anywhere to stalk wild cattle over a difficult mountainous country. It would have been an easy way of getting rid of them, but I preferred, if they must leave the ship, that they should do so by mutual consent, and not by suicide, and steered for the nearest convenient port, which I ascertained rather vaguely from one of the *Shanghai's* charts to be Durban.

I was now well south of the foul current and in the region of the Westerlies, and for three or four days made good progress though the winds were light. There is a fine mark for navigating along here, the heavy confused sea on the edge of the Agulhas current, which I looked at but did not penetrate. What it is like in a westerly gale I shudder to think; we had the calmest weather. Our only excitements were due to fishes and things; one night there was a great panic on deck, P. singing out that we were running on a shoal, he could see the phosphorescence of kelp waving in the swell. Then there was a slight bump, but not such as even the lightest touch on a rock would produce. I rushed on deck and saw the water all afire under us; then the sea parted alongside with a colossal sigh; this shoal that we had hit was only a whale after all, and fortunately not the sort of whale that hits back. Another morning, just as it was getting light, I saw a number of dolphin hanging on the quarter, and got the grains into one of them. I was so much puffed up by this that I abolished fishing lines and stacked the poop with an armoury of spears; and saw no more dolphin, but only porpoises, for which my gear was not strong enough; and when I got a proper harpoon I saw no more porpoises but only whales; and you can't kill a 70-foot fin-back with a 40-foot yacht. So I was no more successful than my other fishermen.

On the 9th of November I suspected that I was somewhere near the coast of Natal, which was behind a black cloud, but knew neither how near nor what part of the coast, for I had no noon sights and distrusted the chronometer. I was just about asking two Norwegian whale-catchers for my position when a squall came along which whisked me away under close reefs and put an end to all communication. It was a pretty heavy squall, though I expect it impressed me by its suddenness as much as by its strength, and very near and continuous thunder and lightning is always rather terrifying; but it was nothing to what they had on shore, and I suppose I was not more than 15 miles off. At Durban there was a whole gale; at Maritzburg the wind blew half the roofs away and hail riddled the rest. What risks the poor landsman does run in bad weather!

The morrow was gloriously fine and the coast of Natal lay clear, 5 miles off, according to the chronometer, but 15 by any reasonable estimate. I think I know what had happened. The optician at Cape Town had (I know this for a fact) let the instrument stop. I suppose he had started it again more or less at haphazard, and falsified the rate in order to conceal the fact that it had been tampered with. There ought to be a specially superheated hell for marine opticians. The moral of that is never to let anyone else touch your chronometer; if you must let it run down then you know that you have done so. If I had gone straight on to Australia and failed to sight Amsterdam Island I should have been some 50 miles out in my reckoning. At noon the sun showed that I was right opposite Port Natal, and the wind came aft and suggested that I should probably get in that evening.

The Port Authorities wanted to make quite certain I got in. At first the signal station reported us as a ship's life-boat—they have an obsession of wrecks since the *Trevessa* business—but were puzzled by our rig; then they saw that we were something bigger, and put us down as a mystery, but always, I suppose, as a possible subject for a salvage claim, for they sent out the biggest tug in the Southern Hemisphere to bring us our pilot. He looked at the wind, which was very light, and at the harbour, which was two or three miles away, and brought a 10-inch hawser with him. I supposed he was anxious about his dinner, and the tug had to get home anyway, so I made fast. I thought it rather sharp practice when I was charged £24 (reduced afterwards to £9) for that tow.

We were tied up for the night alongside a steamer, a very friendly steamer and an habitué of the port, being on the India to South Africa run, the captain of which invited us to use his ship as our own, and for our further entertainment introduced us to the Royal Natal Yacht Club; and the next morning, being Sunday, commanded his barber to minister to us. I was considerably surprised to see a small Indian manœuvring a large chair down a very long and steep side-ladder; it would have been rather less trouble for us to walk up it, but I suppose he wanted publicity when he planted his victims down on my forecastle. He got it; all the yachts in the port had filed past before operations were finished.

H. had an uncle living in Durban, and the prospect of a permanent job under the Union Government; so observing that the ship's company was suffering from incompatibility of temper, he decided to try his luck ashore. I have very often since blamed myself for helping him towards this decision. P. got a friend to sponsor him, so I did not have to put down his passage-money home when I discharged him. There were left *Saoirse* and myself out of this once hopeful expedition.

When I was designing her I remembered that the most probable and the most serious accident that can happen to a yacht is that her crew should desert her in a foreign port. Any substitutes one can pick up will be both expensive and uncongenial; therefore a poor man's boat or a boat so small that one cannot get away from undesirables should be capable of being worked single-handed. So I called her *Saoirse*, signifying in Gaelic "Freedom" and implying that in any reasonable emergency I was free to do what I liked with her, without being under a compliment or indebted to anyone. Then came the question, "Was this a reasonable emergency?" I had envisaged the possibility of getting stranded at Tenerife, but not at Port Natal. But I could easily make it a reasonable emergency; I could surely, now the summer was coming on, get a hand to go to Table Bay with me, a passage I should not have cared to do alone, and I would just as soon sail home single-handed from Table Bay as from Tenerife. It would be rather coming back with my tail between my legs, but it might be enough of a "stunt" to excuse my abandonment of purpose. I tossed up a sixpence and said, "Heads I go on, tails I turn back."

I let it be known that I wanted a crew, and did various small jobs while I was waiting for them, the most important of which was lengthening the spindle of the steering gear so that the helmsman can stand behind the wheel, which makes for better steering in heavy weather, or reach it from the chart-room, which makes for more comfortable steering when it rains. And I got docked and painted free; one would say a whole gaol-full of convicts were turned on to do the painting. I don't think I could live in a country that depended so much on cheap or coloured labour; I want to do the jobs myself, and there you can't. Nor should I feel quite happy about living in a country that did not belong to me but to the Kaffirs. I was not conscious of this feeling at the Cape, where time has softened the crudity of conquest, and so many of the coloured people are Malays anyway. Durban is a paradise for the visitor, but I am glad I am not a resident. It looked, however, as if I had swallowed the anchor, so slow was a crew in appearing.

Then a very young youth came down and camped on board, and forthwith a south-westerly gale began. I was lying head to wind alongside a jetty, with an anchor and plenty of lines out. But I did not know Durban, and the lines were not long enough; the yacht gave two plunges and broke everything, sunk two lighters and drove ashore; and was very smartly hauled off and re-moored by the water police. It was a Sunday night and there was no one about to ask where our lines and fenders came from. No great damage was done, but the very young youth disappeared, and I had to do more waiting.

I was getting nervous about leaving the ship, or I should have gone to Pretoria to see how much better South African town architecture is than British town architecture in South Africa. Fortunate country that in this modern welter of eclecticism can boast a distinctive national tradition of building! I believe it is no tradition at all, but quite a modern invention; still it looks like a tradition and is just as spontaneous. I wonder very much if the Australians will invent anything as characteristic to build Canberra with.

I had been nearly a month in Durban when two more likely customers came along. They had been ordinary

seamen in a Parsee-owned barque that had been seized
for debt in Rangoon, so I supposed they would not have
any very exalted ideas on the subject of comfort or ease,
and signed them on, and got my clearance. At the
last moment a third hand, another very young youth,
was shanghaied on board by his father, who said, quite
untruthfully, that the boy wanted to run away to sea,
and that he, the father, wanted to be sure that he ran
away in a well-managed ship. With such compliments,
and with a thinly veiled anxiety to get rid of his family,
did he suggest to me the rôle of hired assassin; in view of
this and the fact that the boy was evidently so anxious to
get away from his father that he would even ship in a
wind-jammer, I signed him on also, lest the next captain approached might have more literal ideas on the
subject of assassination than I.

Being, therefore, in all respects ready for sea, on the
10th of December, just a month after I had towed in, I
towed out of Port Natal, with a clearance for Lyttelton,
but by now rather late for the prospect of going on from
Lyttelton towards Mount Cook.

CHAPTER V

THE INDIAN OCEAN

THANK God I had got to sea again at last! I had a very pleasant time at Durban, and did not feel that I had outstayed my welcome; but after a month in any one place one wants to have an occupation there. I was so much rejoiced at getting clear of the land that I did not inquire too critically about the means I adopted for getting away. The ship indeed I knew to be in better condition than ever before, but of the crew I knew nothing, except that the two ordinary seamen could do fairly competently such small sailorizing jobs as I had set them while in harbour, and that the boy could not. He therefore became cook and steward, while the other two and I kept watches. Whether because they were by nature easy-going, or because they had been well disciplined in the Parsee barque, or because the wages I was paying were so small that they did not encourage individual opinions, this passage was by far the most comfortable time I had till I was homeward bound from Pernambuco. It was not exciting; they seldom spoke to me, and my one-sided attempts at conversation were rather futile. They were not paid to think, therefore they did exactly what I told them to, and never made the same mistake twice. It was like sailing a ship full of fool-proof machinery single-handed, a most restful occupation compared with the management of people who thought they could sail the ship too. But it was so restful that I have only the vaguest memories of the whole passage, and the two deck hands have passed out of my mind like ghosts. The only incident that I can remember is that I offered the elder of them a 50 per cent. rise of wages and the rating of bosun, and he refused it; which was perhaps as well for all concerned, for as things were it was the most peaceful ship imaginable; there was only one angry word spoken on the passage; and that would have been sorrowful rather than angry had I known that I was subsequently going to see a certificated captain do the very thing that had annoyed me. I paid more attention to the boy, to whom I was, I suppose, *in loco parentis*. He was at bottom a very good boy, but had been badly brought up, at least since he had been in Natal, for he was English. He had never been kicked by anyone except his unnatural parent, and showed the lack of it. He was not very robust or healthy-looking, and I rather wondered what I should make of him after he had got over his sea-sickness. To make a long story short I made, I say, the best helmsman I ever had on board; and he said, when I last saw him working at a good job in Melbourne, that I had made a man of him. I want to take credit for the only good turn I ever did anyone.

But it must be admitted that I did not make much of a sea-cook of him; that is to say, a small-boat cook. Perfection in this is perhaps rarer than in any other art; the aspirant must first of all have been so thoroughly brought up in small boats that he can perform any operation equally well whichever way up the vessel happens to be; and people so brought up seldom have the chance of experiencing much culinary refinement, and if they have done so by such an unlikely event as, for instance, a fisherman becoming apprenticed to a chef, they turn up their noses at the rather primitive equipment of such a yacht as mine. Of course the best of yacht hands at home are all one could desire; but if there is anyone of the sort in the Colonies I never met him. I found one treasure later, who never upset anything; but my poor boy had a genius that way. He managed to make the most superlative grease-slide across the galley, and slid along it into the saloon and generously lubricated that, and then fell down the companion ladder with the slush-bucket and pinched his toe in the biting part of the swinging table; and last of all looked to me for sympathy —and did not get much.

I had started from Dublin with no two ends to the ship, and no provision for making them, so I had to go on from Durban with everyone in the wardroom mess; and with most of my many crews this was unobjectionable. But it is rather a risky experiment, and apart from any social problems I think part of a captain's authority depends on his being remote and unapproachable; I do not recommend this as a general practice.

I knew little more about the best course to steer towards New Zealand, and the advice I had got from other captains in Durban was not very encouraging, and often contradictory; the general conclusion that I drew was that I should get all the wind I wanted in lat. 38° S. One of my gossips told me that he had said this to a friend of his, and when they met at Melbourne the latter had lost his foretopmast and main topgallantmast while my informant made a good passage farther north; that was all the wind that anyone wanted, and a little more; it was a stupid story, because one can get dismasted anywhere outside the Trade Wind zone, and, besides, he didn't tell me what time of the year it was. He also pointed out to me a ship at anchor in the harbour that had her bows turned round and looking aft, after a collision with an iceberg not far from the Cape. The effect of all this was to discourage me from being in too much of a hurry to get to the southward.

We had a good shove off the land for a hundred miles or so, and then ran into a rough sea and trouble with the winds. Either it was calm, or there was so much sea that we could not run anywhere near our proper course, and very slowly at that. I kept looking at the barometer, drawing diagrams on the chart, and racking my brain to discover if there was any section of the Laws of Storms applicable to my present predicament, and if so what was the proper way of dealing with it. Eventually I concluded that the barometer was darkening counsel, for it had not moved for five days, and it must surely be very unusual in these latitudes (32° to 35° S.) to have absolutely no indication of the daily range for a whole week.

At this stage, influenced no doubt by the advice that I had received, I made a very great mistake in my navigation, the same indeed as I had made in the Atlantic, but with less excuse, for here I had a means of escape to the southward. I should have disregarded the advice, the wind, the barometer, and the direction of Australia; kept in the Agulhas current, and drifted with it a hundred miles a day, more or less, to the south-westward. True I did not exactly want to go to the westward, but I had to get to the southward somehow; and once in 37° S. or thereabouts I should make up the lost easting in no time. I imagined that I should get good winds in 37° because I got them there when I came round from Table Bay to Durban, but nothing useful to the north of that latitude;

this was, however, a month nearer midsummer, and I might be disappointed. Anyway I was going to take a monstrous time getting even that far by trying to steer to the south-eastward, for I was by no means succeeding in getting in that direction. I have often preached that the only way to make a passage is to go out of one's way to look for the wind one wants, but I fear I do not always practise what I preach.

When these light winds were accompanied by a confused swell the mainsail had to come in, for the sideways movement of the ship swung it so that it never presented the correctly curved surface to the pressures that impinged on it. At such times even when closehauled we depended on the foresail and the two foretopsails; aided, of course, by two jibs, a mizzen staysail, and the mizzen, which, being less lofty than the mainsail, and to some extent steadied by its boom, did not slam about so much. With the yard hard against the backstays and the bowlines well hauled out, the foresail did good work six points off the wind. But the baggy little topsails, with their long unstiffened leaches, stayed bunted out right into the wind at apparently impossible angles, and did better work still; a property of very light canvas which deserves serious consideration when one is designing a sail plan specially for deep-sea work.

Such a design will, I think, assume that the square sails are the important ones. They are obviously the economical ones, for yards which will stay put when the ship rolls are easier on their gear than gaffs and booms which swing about. There is no reason why they should not be as efficient as fore-and-afters on any practicable point of sailing. A working foresail, if the rigging of the foremast is designed with this end in view and the question of a square topsail disregarded (as in a boat of this size it should be), will set five points off the wind, and no one in their senses would try to sail very far on such a course. The sail must not be too deep, or it will need bowlines, which are a nuisance; also its foot must be a good height above the deck, to make a fair curve outside the rigging. This cramps its size; but when the sheets are eased off to a fair wind there will be plenty of room to lace a useful bonnet under it.

This excellent sail cannot, however, be used in narrow waters or in squally weather, when it might be dangerous to get taken aback, so the ship must carry a sufficient working rig apart from it. A gaff sail will not set on the same mast, as the suction of its luff draws the two together and spoils both. The short-tack rig, then, will be a staysail schooner's; and prudence will dictate a moderate sized mainsail, while deep-sea conditions make a large and light topsail more valuable than an extension of heavy canvas.

This sort of sailing had of course been finding out the weak spots in my running gear (the steady breeze in Table Bay did not try it so hard) and there were large demands on some very nice new hemp rope that I had got in Durban. The next month would be no time for economy, when a parted sheet might mean the loss of a sail. Then I began to look out some clothes for the bad weather; for though I was not going farther south than Lisbon is north and it was midsummer, it is never warm at sea when the wind blows. The clothes were found all right, but, alas! there was not a button left on them. For a long time I was puzzled by the absence of those buttons, till I remembered that they were made of casein, and that casein was the substance of cheese, and that cheese was the food of rats, and that I had a rat on board, though I had not troubled much about him hitherto for he appeared to live on deck and on a diet of raw onions. I confirmed his guilt when I bought a rat-trap in Melbourne, for I baited it with a button and killed him. I wished now I had some means of dealing with him. I had been offered a mongoose by the mate of a big Belgian training-ship—a four-masted barque—in Durban, but I refused him because the rat had not then come on board, and besides I could not catch the mongoose. He was supposed to live in the sheave-hole in the foretopmast, but if he did he would not come out for all my blandishments.

On the 21st of December the barometer at last started to go down, we reached the 36th parallel, and we picked up a breeze of wind which in spite of a rough sea gave us a run of 150 miles to the following noon. But it had no staying power, and a monstrous big swell prevented our getting any farther to the southward until the 27th, when the wind backed to the east and gave us another degree of latitude. But then, from being east, which I did not mind, though it was accompanied by an abominably steep sea, for I wanted to get still farther south, it went to the south-east, more wind, more sea, and heavy rain; none of which things I liked at all. But if I could not make the weather comfortable I made myself comfortable; I hove-to, and had a good long night in bed, which I purchased at the cost of a day's work of 17 miles in the wrong direction. But that was not a great matter. After, if not because of, this rest, we proceeded to a week of 140-mile runs. I am by no means sure that a slack day every now and then does not pay. One takes it of course without calculating when there is a head wind and nothing else to do; in this case, for instance, all the indications were that I should get a fair wind soonest by staying where I was; but in these latitudes, where calms or very light winds do not last long, it is perhaps a mistake to spend on pulley-hauling of topsail halliards and sheets the energy which would be better employed in carrying sail on days when sail will get one somewhere. Another precept which I do not practise, for I have a restless and fidgety nature, and find it hard to sit down and enjoy a fine day.

I kept on within a few miles either side of the 37th parallel until the 4th of January, 1924, when I went a little farther south to look for Amsterdam Island. I did not go there only to shoot wild cattle, or to look at the view, or to rescue castaways, or because I had a sentimental affection for the last milestone on the road to the Antipodes; I went primarily to check the rate of my chronometer. It seems rather ridiculous to divide a run of only fifty days into two periods of twenty-five for this purpose, but I had been told so often that a chronometer would not keep its rate in a small boat that I had regarded mine with suspicion; and since I had only one of them I had no means of telling whether it was going properly except by confirming the positions of islands and the like or by observing lunar distances. And when it comes to working lunars, as I did before making the land at the Cape, I think they suffer from the violent motion a great deal more than any chronometer.

That morning was not recommended for astronomical observations; it was thick with rain, and the ghost of a sun which rarely appeared was little use in the virtual absence of any horizon. However, the weather was not so thick nor the wind and sea so high at the time that I was afraid of hitting the island by daylight, and as I ought to see it early in the afternoon I steered straight for it. I do not usually like to run down wind towards any land in thick weather, but I knew this particular land was quite small, quite round, and quite clear of dangers. I had hardly realized the existence of Amsterdam Island till I got to Durban, when a friend to whom I was talking at the ship-chandler's said, for my benefit, I presume, that there was a store of provisions and clothing for shipwrecked mariners there. On my asking for further information the ship-chandler produced, to my astonishment, a whole drawer-full of charts of Amsterdam and St. Paul's Islands; large-scale things that showed every stone and hot spring of them and were surrounded with pretty pictures. When I expressed my astonishment, he said so many vessels were lost between the Cape and Australia that anyone who found himself reasonably near the Islands called there for castaways, and he sold them the charts so that they should know where to look for distress signals and landing-places.

St. Paul's is the more interesting in the pictures; it is a breached volcanic crater with a bottomless lake in the middle, into which one can pull a boat, and any amount of hot springs; but the only livestock appear to be penguins; anyway it was 70 miles farther south than I was going. Amsterdam is also a volcano, but quite extinct, and of the convex kind; it has no harbours, but is said to abound with cattle and cabbages.

At noon I was, according to my reckoning, 30 miles from the island, and approaching it at the rate of $6\frac{1}{2}$ knots. At twenty minutes past one I saw, high up in the sky above the smother along the water, a streak of black, becoming more defined and lenticular in shape; then the right-hand point was cut off by a patch of light which, advancing with a clear-cut vertical front, rapidly swallowed up the remainder, but before the last of the dark wedge had vanished, hung a little speck of black in front of it. What I had seen was obviously the upper part of a cliff in profile with the top of a rocky pinnacle standing near it, but I had not the least idea how far off it was.

There are few people who, if told while at sea to look for the top of a hill 2,000 feet high, will look for it in anything like the right direction. Personally I always look somewhere near the horizon, and every time I wonder afresh how the thing gets such an absurd distance up in the air. I get so much accustomed to limiting my view to a few minutes of arc above the visible horizon, that is the water, wherever it may be, for to me on my low deck a very ordinary sea will encroach on many degrees of sky, and yet I have no difficulty in seeing the top of it. I can only guess roughly, for I had no opportunity of measuring the thing, that what I saw might have been 100 feet of cliff 5 miles away, or 400 feet 20 miles away, as improbable extremes; or anything in between. There was not evidence enough here to convict a dollar watch of perjury, let alone a very reputable chronometer. So I had failed in my primary object. It was also obvious that I was going to fail to see any view, or to shoot any cattle, and one can sentimentalize over the ideal far better than over the visible image of a milestone. It was my duty, however, if I could rediscover the island, to look for castaways; and I therefore carried on, though the weather was getting thicker and the wind and sea no less. I went up and sat on the foreyard for a couple of hours—you gentlemen that perch precariously on cross-trees do not know how comfortable it is to have a nice substantial foresail sticking out in front of you to keep your legs from dangling—for the first thing I should see would probably be the surf along the shore, and though as the visibility had now decreased to about a mile, as I should guess, and the surf could be seen as soon from the deck, only from aloft could one tell at all the trend of the coast, or which way to steer to go clear of it. But either my helmsman was careless, or, as is more probable, I had set an unnecessarily wide course, for I never saw the land again; and to tell the truth, as the weather was getting thicker all the time, and it was impossible that the castaways should have seen me, I was very glad to miss it. Of course the next day was gloriously fine; this, and that day the previous week that we had spent hove-to, were the only really bad days of the whole passage.

Here I saw a dead penguin floating in the water, a thing, you will say, that might happen to any penguin and was hardly worth comment. But it puzzled me that he should be floating there in this hungry Southern Ocean, and not inside the stomach of an albatross. For albatrosses eat salt beef, bread and jam, and raw potatoes, therefore why not penguins? and penguins are eaten by skua-gulls and by seals, therefore why not by albatrosses? I looked over the stern to see if our albatross would be diverted from the very meagre contents of the slush-bucket to a tasty piece of fresh meat; and lo, our albatross was not there. That one I knew by the fact that he had three white feathers in a line on his port wing, and four in a diamond on his starboard, and he had followed us for 600 miles. He may have felt tired, though it is said that these birds sleep while on the wing; or he may have had an establishment on Amsterdam Island, and turned aside on urgent private affairs; but why were there no others in his place? Can it be that albatrosses do not eat penguins; and if so, what do they eat? They cannot dive after fish, they will not take a slice of bread if you hold it a foot above the water, and the amount of food which is to be found actually floating is negligible. Yet they are big birds and must take a lot of feeding. And the same question might be asked, and I cannot suggest an answer, in the case of all the larger gulls; very small birds like Mother Carey's chickens no doubt can live on the minute organisms which inhabit the top layer of the sea, but one cannot imagine an albatross subsisting on plankton.

Last week's run had come to 982 miles, and it looked as if I had really at last struck the right conditions for pulling up our deplorable average from Durban; but not yet. Even here in $37\frac{1}{2}°$ S. I had a day of calms, and logged 55 miles only, but in the evening a little breeze from the N.N.E., which is the best wind for making passages, sprang up. From noon of the 7th of January the ship began to get her favourite weather, a moderate beam wind with a smooth sea.

A far better index of the state of the wind and the sea than any mere numbers or conventional words, is an account of the work which was going on on board at the time, remembering the size of the yacht and the fact that she had only twenty-three inches of freeboard. The considerable amount of carpentry and joinery done are immaterial: I made blocks for the foretopsail halliards and lockers for my cabin mainly in the chart-room, which is of such dimensions that one can chock off both oneself and one's work in almost any weather; I never broke a brace bit, and only one hack-saw blade, in these circumstances. But I wanted a smooth sea to dissect the chart-room clock, clean it, and assemble it so that it would go. I wanted a smooth sea to put three sacks of coal into the bunker, for the opening was in the lowest part of the lee side of the deck. With the smooth sea the wind was not entirely a calm; with every sail in the ship set we ran 163 miles up to noon of the 18th.

Next day there was a little more wind, consequently a little more sea, and therefore, as was the general rule, our run was 7 miles less. So after noon I took in the fore-topsail. During the morning of the 19th we finished putting new seizings throughout on the port ratlines and got them nicely square for going into harbour, and tarred down the rigging that side. The absence of that foretopsail made a difference of half a knot; this day we did 168 miles. And after noon there was a little more wind, but the sea was regular and easy, and I took in the gaff-topsail, and because the ship did not roll or lurch, but just rose and fell as the long round-topped waves passed under her, I boomed out the sails with boat-hooks and oars so as to get the very greatest efficiency from them, a thing that can seldom be done without breaking the boat-hooks. And next morning, after a night that might have been spent in harbour except for a slight list, we were very busy overhauling and re-stowing stores, and broaching the salt beef and putting it into the harness cask; and at noon the log showed 175 miles. And that was a very comfortable way of getting through four days and 660 miles of the Southern Ocean and a useful amount of work.

But in the evening the wind began to blow and we began to reef, and in spite of all the ship began to go more slowly and could not do any better than 145 miles by noon of the 12th. The wind was backing towards the north-west, but even so we were well content with jib, foresail, and close reefed mainsail. And this evening we nearly lost the foresail, for the eye on the cathead which had been made in Cape Town to take the foretack carried away. Now I have got the iniquities of Cape Town off my mind; for any future accidents I was more directly responsible.

The barometer was falling more and more rapidly, and it was clear that the depression which had been gradually overtaking us for the last six days had arrived. We could not go any faster, to keep ahead of it; if I had tried to set any more sail I should only have lost it, for a gale was blowing. Either the trough of the storm was moving irregularly, or it had well-developed secondaries attached, for after a night from the south-west the wind ran back to the north-west next morning, still of gale force, and making a very rough sea of it. It was time to look out for squalls, so I took in the mainsail and kept my eyes open; and sure enough before long the wind flew back to the south-west and began blowing very hard. I was not at all prepared for what I saw. That wind just tore blocks out of the long ridges of the north-westerly sea, piled Pelion on Ossa and the resulting pyramid on top of the huge south-westerly swell that runs without ceasing round the Southern Ocean, often unnoticed, but rising in an instant at the touch of its normal wind; and the result was stupendous. I do not suppose it very often happened that all three sets of waves climbed up each other's backs, but it happened

once within a ship's length of me. Of course the elevation of 40 feet, as I judged it to be, was quite moment-
ary; the pile was entirely top-heavy and the upper 10
feet or so curled over as clean as if it had tripped up on a
reef and tumbled all over the ocean. You need not believe it, but that is what it looked like. Where then was
the storm-oil? In the forepeak, and it would have taken
dangerously long to get it out. Where then was the sea
anchor? In a mess; at least the gear was; it would have
taken impossibly long to clear it. Why then did I not
heave-to? Well, we did not make that sea break, and if it
wanted to break over us it would do so quite irrespec-
tive of which end on we lay to it, or whether we were
sailing or stopped, and that would be the end of the
story either way; so I thought I would make all speed
out of that dangerous locality, and carried on in the
direction of Australia at the very surprising speed—seeing that we generally do so poorly in a gale—of $7\frac{1}{2}$
knots. The wind blew so hard that by noon it had flat-
tened all the irregularities off the true swell, which was
now immensely big, but long and easy. I put down 170
miles in the log and hoped for another day as good on
the morrow.

But I was disappointed. The wind became lighter
and the sea more irregular again, and the day's run was
no more than 153 miles; this making 1,130 for the week,
an average of 6·8 knots, allowing that the week was an
hour and a half short on account of the change of longitude. It was considerably the best week's run I ever did,
and rather unexpectedly so, seeing that it included three
days of gales. I sometimes wonder whether it was because these were the best helmsmen I ever had. If they
were, it is attributable to the fact that none of them had

ever been in steam. For your steamboat quartermaster, and to a certain extent the helmsman of a big ship, imagines that the compass is placed in front of him to steer by, whereas one cannot keep up with the swing of the ship by the most violent efforts to follow the most lively compass card. The boy especially, because he had never steered by compass in his life, learned very soon to judge his course from the breath of the wind on his neck, and to balance himself in such a way that he unconsciously anticipated each swing of the ship's head from her heave and roll. Or perhaps the seas were not really as bad as I thought they were; always excepting that portentous breaker. That did me a lot of harm; it lost my best helmsman for me, for when it came along the boy was not in his bunk or in the galley, but had come on deck to look at the pretty view—in the Southern Hemisphere it is the south-west wind that clears up the weather—and he saw that breaker and swore he would go to sea no more. This was the only indication I ever had from any of my crews that my ship was at all smaller than the average; and even this was not a very clear indication, for it was the size of the sea that he objected to. It was rather touching to see the way in which they all took for granted my infallibility as well as that of the ship; in some cases it made for carelessness, but this crowd were so conscientious that even when I logged strong gales I do not remember having done more than my usual share of watch-keeping.

The past week was not only my fastest, but also my straightest run; I never went north of 37° 50′ S., or south of 38° 20′, which is rather remarkable in view of the heavy sea. But courses are pure chance; next day I found myself 70 miles to the northward, in this manner.

On the afternoon of the 14th it was blowing very hard again, and the ship was rolling catastrophically, and partly, I admit, through curiosity, to see how it was done, and partly because I thought it was asking rather much of the canvas to keep the whole of it set, I put a reef in the foresail. It is a sound maxim to let well alone. Certainly I learned how to put in the reef, after trying to do it in a variety of wrong ways, but while the chain jackstay, on which the yard is hoisted or lowered, was temporarily slack, the pin securing it to tne parrel must have worked loose, for during the night it dropped out. So long as I kept the lifts and braces taut nothing would carry away; the misfortune was that the yard was quite square and I did not dare to touch the braces when the wind went round to the south-west again, but had to run away off my course. Not till the afternoon had the sea come down enough for me to go aloft and remedy matters. I turned out that reef, and never used it again.

A deplorable reaction followed on this glorious week. The first symptom was the omission to set the mainsail, on the grounds that the ship was rolling too heavily. Reviewing critically my log-book—a thing that I have no right to do, for it cannot record all the circumstances nor can I remember them—I suggest that the ship was rolling so heavily because the mainsail was not set. At any rate there was enough wind to blow the clew out of the jib, and we, the arm-chair critics, suppose that would be enough to keep the mainsail full; only light winds could justify my taking it in, and depending on an inadequate square-sail. At any rate my last ten days to Australia were nothing to be proud of. I imagine one works best with a little opposition; left to myself I am too quick to reduce and too slow to make sail, and on this passage I was left to myself; but when on a subsequent passage I had a man always clamouring for reefs my natural retort was to set the topsails.

I found a use for the fine weather, however. I remembered that all civilization is built on a basis of slavery, and having for the first time slaves, and willing ones, at my disposal, I started to civilize the ship with holystones, brass polish, and like implements. The good and steady southerly wind, if not the best from the Navigator's point of view, was a godsend from the Mate's; it enabled me to get the starboard rigging rattled down and tarred. As a final gesture I scraped and oiled the skylights, deck houses, and other bright work, which started innumerable leaks, but on this occasion I cared more for smartness (I need hardly say that I painted them all over before venturing on the cold and stormy Pacific) and was congratulated by the Melbourne pilot on my yacht-like appearance.

In the morning of the 29th I made the land all along the beam, and saw the first vessel for fifty days. It was a very featureless coast, but, seeing how many vessels make their landfall hereabouts, it might well be better described in the Sailing Directions. However, by assuming the chronometer to be correct, I decided that I was off Warrnambool, and set a course for Cape Otway.

Five years ago there must have been magnificent scenery along here, with a forest of huge trees coming right down to the water's edge over the tumbled cliffs of Moonlight Head. But looking at the bare grassy promontory I was passing, I wondered if this could be Moonlight Head or if I were miles adrift in my reckoning, till I saw a few bare poles standing up on the skyline far inland. The whole place had been ravaged by a fire of such severity that near the coast even the trunks of the trees had fallen. But there are still plenty of trees in Victoria; long before I reached Cape Otway at night-fall I was passing dense woodland, and next morning all the country that I could see was covered with forest as far as the summit of the Otway Range; for we drifted slowly up that coast to Port Phillip.

Why, oh why, was I drifting towards Port Phillip when I was bound for Port Lyttelton? I was short of bacon, baking-powder, and potatoes. I had a peculiarly beastly breakfast of vegetarian cutlets which I had com-pounded principally of peas and oatmeal, for by bad management there were no scraps of salt beef available this morning; and in any case it would have been un-enterprising to be only a mile away from Australia and not drop in and spend a week-end there. So I drifted right up to Port Phillip Heads with the pilot signal flying, and at two o'clock the pilot came on board, just a little annoyed because he was waiting to take in the 20,000-ton *Mooltan*. She, however, was unfortunately a day late, as does happen to steamboats on their maiden voyages; and we were three days early, for this was only Wednesday, and our usual practice is to arrive on a Saturday.

We were rushed past the signal station on a boiling flood-tide, flying a hoist of flags for which neither I nor the International Code was responsible, but which the pilot said would expedite the arrival of the doctor to give us pratique when we got to Hobson's Bay. In both Australian and New Zealand ports a code is used which necessitates flags that no foreign vessel has in her locker, and the yellow flag, the most important of all, which in every other country signifies a request for pratique, here has another meaning. They call this being independent; but they are careful to add that the International Code will be understood. I hoped the doctor would get that signal, for there was not much wind, and we should get up so late that there would be a poor chance of finding him that night, and if we did not the unlucky pilot would be stuck on board. My crew did their best to get the ship along, and, no doubt anxious to show off before the Colonials, surpassed themselves in setting and trimming sail. One is proud of the appreciation of a Melbourne pilot, and we had the senior pilot of the port, for they are all sailing ship captains and the youngest of them knows how things ought to be done, while the elder have handled the yacht-like clippers of the racing wool fleet and know how things really were done in the days when there were crews to do them. So it was good to see one of my hands, without any suggestion from me, laying out to the yard-arm—and there is no footrope— to take a turn out of the clew of the foretopsail. And in case we did not get ashore that night it was also good to see that the cook had saved half a dozen potatoes and was struggling with a French dictionary to find out the proper terms in which to describe the five courses which he proposed to serve for dinner. If he could not do as well as the chef of the *Mooltan* he was going to do as well as he could.

It was seven o'clock before we passed the Gellibrand Pile Light, and then we passed two ships at anchor; real ships, that is, square-rigged on all three masts; we had come to a port where the business of the sailor is understood, and where not quite everybody asks one how one managed without a motor. It was half-past seven when we anchored, just opposite the place where the earliest emigrants landed before Melbourne was a city, to find, of course, that the doctor was not available; but I hope I consoled Captain P. for not bringing in the largest vessel that had ever come into Melbourne by entertaining him in a style which he did not expect in the smallest vessel that had ever come into Melbourne from a foreign port.

CHAPTER VI

AUSTRALIA AND NEW ZEALAND

I was not long in scraping acquaintance with the yachts-men of Melbourne. Early on Sunday morning, my crew being still ashore and I without a boat, I started to drag my anchor and scraped up against most of the yachts in Williamstown. My numerous rescuers, moved no doubt by anxiety for their own boats as much as for mine, offered me a handsome choice of moorings, and every other sort of hospitality. My crew came back, with the necessary bacon and potatoes, and all seemed ready for a start on the morrow.

But I do not get to sea as easily as that. At first dawn I got up, went to shake up the cook, and put my hand on emptiness. So were the other two bunks empty, and the boat was gone. A large trunk, a bag, and a coat or two were in evidence, so at first I supposed that my crew would come back before long, especially as none of them was very well provided with money. I had divided the total cash on board into five parts; one for each of us and one for the ship, and it was only £7 10s. to begin with. Later in the morning I noticed that the bag had collapsed; I looked inside, and found it empty. The trunk was empty. The coats were the kind one usually throws overboard at the end of a passage. The crew had deserted. It was annoying, for I was already a month behind my time, and every day lost was out of the middle of the climbing season. I reported to the shipping office as soon as I could communicate with the shore, but that was not very soon. One would expect to see men and boats about early on a Monday morning in a yachting harbour at midsummer, but I expected in vain. One might hope for someone on shore that could read signals, but I had almost given up hope before anything happened. One learns patience in the Antipodes; I was worse marooned at Auckland.

This was now the 4th of February; it was only a fortnight's run to New Zealand, and I had no doubt that I could get a crew for that, even if I had to wait a day or two and pay rather fantastic wages. But I had forgotten the Press. To the journalist a plain account of a job quietly and efficiently done is not a story; he wants battle, murder, and sudden death. So one attributed to me a tale of tempest which stamped the writer as a very timid or very inexperienced person; and another represented me as backing every order with a loaded revolver. It was no wonder the decent sort of crews fought shy of me. It is true that my late leading hand stated to an interviewer that he had no complaint of my character, of the ship's seaworthiness, or of the nature of the voyage; but that he was getting twice the wages in Melbourne that he was likely to get in London. But that interview did not appear in the papers that circulate most on the water-front.

I did of course get a certain number of applicants for a berth, mostly people who had never been to sea but who had good reason for getting out of Australia. There was also such a plague of remittance-men looking for free drinks that I grew to distrust anyone wearing good clothes and speaking English. Most of my encounters with these gentry were merely squalid; one was amusing. A soi-disant Lord S. wanted to carry me off to dinner in an opulent-looking motor-car, in which were two other men. Now from references in conversation to mutual acquaintances I had identified Lord S. within a first cousinship or so, and I knew that the seat of the family was S.; but I was not sufficiently up to date in the peerage to know whether such a title existed. It was possible, however, so I got into the car and we started for Melbourne. It soon transpired that the owner of the car knew nothing about his passenger, and shortly afterwards Lord S. said he had dropped a five-pound note in the car and could not find it. Then we, growing suspicious, stunned him with cocktails and drove him to the police-station instead of to the hotel. When searched he had not the price of one dinner on him, let alone of four; and next day he was jailed for bilking a taxi-driver. I do not think it was fair of the papers to represent him as a friend of mine without adding that I had delivered to justice a man for whom the police had been looking for six weeks.

But the Melbourne police were at the time inexperienced and handicapped by a wave of crime following the strike and dismissal of their predecessors, and even human life was pretty cheap. I had given a man who was absolutely down and out, but who was a decent honest man when he was sober, a couple of days at rigging work, and paid him for them, intending to sign him on the ship's articles next day. Admittedly he spent his wages unwisely, but he was the kind of man who would always turn up on time if he were alive, so I was rather anxious when he did not. Four days later I was sent for to identify his drowned body. The coroner of course returned an open verdict, without calling as witnesses any of the people who had last seen him. I do not necessarily suggest foul play, but there was nothing to disprove its possibility.

At a later time, when my yacht was in dock in a rather unhealthy neighbourhood, and I was having dinner at Fasoli's, the man who was sitting next to me, and whom I found out to be a police inspector, said: "If you are going down Dudley Street to-night don't carry that gun in your pocket; carry it in your hand, where they can see it." For the city is not so bad that robbers dare to use anything noisier than a sandbag; if after a row one is found with a smoking revolver in one's hand it is prima-facie evidence of innocence.

A week after I had lost my old crew the Shipping Master found me a new lot. When I signed them on everyone in the Shipping Office was unexpectedly cordial, and, it seemed to me, unnecessarily anxious to get me away to sea. I did not then know why, and duly sailed with three Tasmanians. The weather was fine and the wind light, but southerly, and the rip off Port Phillip Heads, where a 7-knot tide runs over a rocky bottom, was in first-class working order. It laid out two of my hands with sea-sickness, instanter; and the third became nearly as green with fright. I hoped that when we reached the smooth water outside they would distinguish themselves in some other way, but they did not. They did nothing; they could do nothing; when they had stopped being sick they expected me to materialize a cook for them, in the middle of Bass Straits! I did something quite as effective; I found a head wind and a sea which was, if possible, worse than what one gets between Dublin and Caergybi. They talked no more of cooks. After drifting round Bass Straits for a couple of days (I could not get out, for the weather was very thick, as well as windy) all three decided they had had enough, and asked me to take them home. I had had more than enough of them and did so. When I went into the Shipping Office to pay them off the atmosphere was despondent. I heard one man say, "I didn't think he'd get far with that crew," followed by a low chorus of, "But why did he bring them back?" Well, I think the Shipping Master might have dropped a rather broader hint to a stranger that manslaughter was indicated. It might have been committed had I known that those Tasmanian devils had walked off with a gold watch and one or two other souvenirs of some intrinsic value. But this is only one side of Melbourne, and I suppose I could be robbed as well in the Commercial Road as in Flinders Street.

Elsewhere I discovered a friendly country, though unfortunately I could not explore it far. (The only night I spent on shore was that on which my man was drowned.) The most interesting people that I met were the owner of the yacht *Seaweed*, a boat of about the same size as mine, which had left Southampton a fortnight and reached Melbourne a month before I did, and his wife; and they had only one man with them; but the same man all the way, which accounted perhaps for their quicker passage, for I lost just a month in Durban, to say nothing of what I lost by light and variable winds going to and coming from that port. The other yachtsmen that I met at Williamstown were extremely helpful, for they were sea-going cruiser-men, and knew what I wanted. At that time two of them were building new yachts, more or less of my size and type; one on the spot, and the other in Hobart. My geographical critic will remark that Hobart is nowhere near Melbourne but at the farther end of Tasmania; and so it is, but the Melbourne yachtsmen do not confine themselves to sailing round Port Phillip, which indeed is about the dullest place imaginable, but go all round the Tasmanian coast, and a very beautiful coast it is too. So when one of them criticized my jib sheets, and gave me a pair of chain traces off a dray to replace them (for he was the manager of a brewery), I accepted the criticism and the gift with equal readiness. Everybody gave me things; A. towed me up the river and down again, B. docked me (these are always my first considerations), and so on down the alphabet to the Royal Yacht Club of Victoria; and neither the Pilots nor the Commonwealth nor Victorian Governments, nor the Melbourne Port and Docks Board charged me anything.

And of course the inevitable question was put to me: "What do you think of Australia?" I did not see Australia, but only Melbourne, and my opinion of it was unpopular. I said that I liked the cable cars because they reminded me of Edinburgh, but that Flinders Street did not remind me of Princes Street; and that considering the amount of money piled up in stone and mortar along Collins Street it was singularly unimpressive. But one might say the same about Adderley Street in Cape Town or Queen Street in Auckland, or, I expect, about the principal street in any colonial city. The chief fault of Melbourne, however, is that it is built in the wrong place. It ought to stretch in a huge semicircle round a continuous quay from St. Kilda to Gellibrand Point, and the docks and wharves up the little ditch called the Yarra River should never have been built; even now they have lost much trade to Sandridge and Williamstown. Some day, but not in my lifetime, those two places will join.

But to come back from the city of Melbourne, back with regret from that delightful Italian restaurant of which the owner is half County Clare and the waitresses wholly County Cork, but which differs from an Irish hotel in that a piano stands in the dining-room and as like as not some operatic star who is visiting the town will give a turn after dinner, to my ship and the chances of my voyage. A very pleasant young man called on me, the second mate of a Finnish training-ship, who wanted to sail with me if his captain would let him, for he was in a hurry to get married and his ship was going up the Pacific coast and it was unknown when she would get home. But there was not a chance that his captain would let him go; he could not possibly get out here a substitute with his qualifications of competency, education, and language.

I went on board his ship, as I did on the Belgian training-ship in Durban, and as I might have on two other great four-masted barques, one Finnish and one Danish, here in Melbourne, and I saw one of the things they do better in other countries than mine. Here were 50 to 80 boys getting a good general as well as a first-class nautical education, and probably, for all these vessels were carrying full cargoes and making good passages, costing very little either to their parents or to the State. I say they were getting a good general education, not because they were learning Greek or Philosophy, but because they were learning things generally at first hand, and that is the only good way to learn. It is hard to see things accurately from a mail steamer or a railway train, blinded, as one generally is, by a mist of conventionality and the distorting mirror of printed books; one wants to drop on things unexpectedly with no preconceived ideas. But one must have a mind capable of assimilating new ideas, and that will not be developed except in surroundings rather more cultured than the half-deck of the average tramp. I say nothing as to the destiny of the finished product of these State-aided training-ships, the junior officer, in view of the overcrowded state of the profession, unless it be a prophecy that no boy who considered the sea as his career would go as apprentice in a privately owned ship —a good deal to the advantage of everyone except the ship-owners; but 60 per cent. of those boys will not follow the sea; they went there to see the world and will leave having learned self-reliance and discipline in a way which they could not learn it on shore or on a steamboat.

In the end I secured a crew. First G., a Swedish-American, a soft slow man with a charming smile and an imperturbable temper; a man brought up for the most part in five- and six-masted schooners, no doubt an excellent fellow to work all the gear of his mast with a steam capstan, but altogether too soft and slow for me. He admitted, when we parted at Auckland, that he was no use in so small a vessel and a sore trial to my temper. I was very sorry, for he was an affectionate creature; but what he said was perfectly true. W., the other member of my crew, was a complete contrast; a wiry active man, and a bundle of nerves and complexes. He was of good family and had a good record as an officer, but when he came to me he was eating husks with the swine. He was full of good stories of his adventurous life— except of one episode, which, however, is otherwise re-

corded as one of the heroic tales of the sea. His tempera-
ment was too much like mine for safety, but I was prepared to risk a clash for the sake of having an educated
Englishman to talk to. I killed a fatted calf and wrote a
letter home in which I said that all my troubles were
over except such as were incidental to a winter passage
round the Horn. I am an extremely bad prophet and I
misinterpreted what omens there were. I indulged in a
sort of trial trip, which was only a Sunday afternoon
sail round Hobson's Bay to look at the British Cruiser
Squadron, and forgetting that I had three guests on
board who were doing all the work, I was so much
struck by the smartness with which the ship was handled
that I prophesied a racing passage. It was too late to go
mountaineering in New Zealand, but it would not be
too late for the Horn if I got a good start and passed to
the southward of Stewart Island. So I got a clearance
for Dublin, and sailed.

For a day all went well; then I was stricken down by
some sort of poisoning; a distressing malady, which,
however, saved the ship. For on the night of the first
of April, after passing Goose Island (and who shall say
that in such circumstances something foolish is not likely
to happen?), I set a course, an obviously imprudent
course on such a dark night, for Banks Straits, and went
below. But not for long; my malady compelling me, I
came on deck, went over to the lee rail, and saw a
ghastly pyramid of black rock sticking up well on my
lee bow. Fortunately my mate was quick in action, the
vessel quick on her helm, the wind off shore, and the
water smooth, or the cruise would have ended then and
there on Clarke Island. I did not cut any more corners
fine that night, and I darkened the ship; for the foolish

thing I had done was to leave the gas blazing away in the cabin with the skylight open, so that the helmsman could see nothing; and there was no look-out forward as there should have been in such narrow waters.

As soon as we were clear of the land I decided I was too sick to take any more watches, but the other two were aggressively cheerful and quite prepared to carry on the good work of 150 miles per diem. Unfortunately some one left a fishing line towing astern all night, and at dawn I found that it had hooked and drowned an unfortunate mollymawk, which is a small kind of albatross. Superstition apart, it is an infamous thing to kill an albatross, for they are such friendly birds and one does not have much company in the Southern Ocean; this one of course died an accidental death, but before long retribution descended on the cause of the accident. G. knocked his elbow on a bulkhead, and it swelled up and got sore. We others suffered incidentally, for in a day we were head-reaching under short canvas as uncomfortably as might be expected in the Tasman Sea, which is notoriously the roughest bit of water in the world, and all the time getting driven farther and farther to the northward. However, if one can't pass New Zealand on one side, one must go on the other; there is only about 800 miles of it. By the time a fair wind came along the best course was through the middle of it, through Cook Strait; it would have been undesirable on account of the temptations of the seductive harbours that lie on either side of it, were it not that G.'s arm was becoming worse and it might be necessary to go into one of those harbours for a doctor. I was by now all right again.

We did not lose much time over this part of the pas-

sage and on the 14th day out I took the morning watch
in order to see New Zealand. I was rather anxious about
the stage-managing of this; I might have sailed too slowly
during the night and seen the land only as a pimple on
the horizon, or it might have been less fine, with only a
dark mass showing under a bank of cloud; but it turned
out all right, the clouds were lying low on the water and
high above them the sun was emerging from behind the
colossal cone of Mount Egmont, which I had approached within 40 miles.

I think this was the most impressive mountain scenery
I ever saw. The parabolic sweep of a volcanic cone is a
very beautiful line, but it is commonly rather flat; the
andesite of Egmont, however, forms an unusually steep
curve, and moreover the less interesting 3,000 feet at the
bottom (the whole peak is 8,000 feet) were cut off by the
low mists and the curvature of the globe. Various
causes make a mountain look big; the stark symmetry of
the volcano is one, the complexity of such a system as
Snowdon is another, but the most potent is the contrast
when one sees them standing on another element, such
as the true sea horizon, or a mist lying on a level plain,
so that there is a gap of as many miles as one's imagina-
tion cares to make it between the foreground and the
background. I have admired a great peak 9,000 feet
high all day, and, when I got near, it looked positively
insignificant beyond icebergs and whales and all the
detail of an Antarctic coast-line.

In the course of time I began to see more rather
attractive-looking mountains to the southward, and as
my mate told me that on that side there was a place
somewhat like Glengariff with a hospital (for G. seemed
likely to require hospital treatment), I decided to go

and see if Picton were really anything like the most beautiful place in the world. It wasn't; at Glengariff trees were (I speak of ten years ago) cut judiciously; in New Zealand they are burned indiscriminately: in the few days that I spent at Picton the aspect of the place was quite considerably changed. It is no good having a long memory for places in this country. Most of the North Island is volcanic, and therefore liable to any sort of transposition of the solider features; the Tarawera eruption changed lakes into mountains, ridges into valleys, and destroyed the famous pink and white terraces which used to draw sightseers from all over the world. (It is proposed to reproduce them in concrete, but that will not guarantee their permanence.) The rest is mud, and visited by torrential rains: it is therefore not uncommon to meet rows of houses sliding down the streets of a town. Hence the houses are built of wood, so that they will float on the mud and may easily be salved. At Rotorua there are both volcanoes and mud; it is so typical that they send tourists there to look at it.

But I had not got to any town yet, and was going slowly enough about getting there. There had been floods up the Wanganui River, and Cook Strait was full of floating logs quite heavy enough to do damage and requiring us to keep a good look-out by day and to heave-to at night.

From a distance the aspect of the rugged promontories that enclose Queen Charlotte Sound is not unlike that of the great headlands of West Cork and Kerry, but as I drifted (for the wind was going down with the sun) alongside the cliffs I noticed a considerable difference. Most conspicuously they were far greener than ours. Cape Jackson does not stick out a very long way into any ocean, but I doubt if any point on the Irish coast has grass growing so low down on it. The seas in this part of the world must be much smaller than ours at home; and this part of the world seems to include everything north of the 40th parallel. I made no comment at the time on the statement in the Sailing Directions that Moonlight Head in Victoria, which faces directly the Southern Ocean, was densely wooded to the water's edge, or the fact which I could observe that it is now completely covered with grass, but I should have remarked it; indeed I did not speculate on the relative severity of the weather here and at home till I saw on Little Barrier Island, which I admit is on an east coast, trees actually growing on a few yards of beach between the ocean and the cliffs; and then I said in my ignorance of the Southern Ocean that there was nothing like the North Atlantic. Certainly the North Island of New Zealand is not like it; the things that sail and steam and motor round the coast here would not be allowed to go out of harbour at home. And just here in Cook Strait they hunt whales in racing motor-launches; exactly how they kill the whales I did not learn, but apparently they do not kill themselves.

The grass, however, on Cape Jackson looked coarse and rank, the earth was raw and there were frequent traces of recent landslips; it is a very new country. A little farther on I saw the "bush," which, no doubt owing to the fact that it grows on smooth slopes of clay-rock instead of between ridges of hard slate, is denser in appearance than the virgin forest of Cork or Kerry. Farther on yet I saw another difference from our scenery. These Sounds were not shaped by glacial action but by the wear of many streams on the soft rock; they are not cut clean and straight as are our three great bays, nor are they ruled by anything analogous to the Hercynian master-folds; they wander about like any river valley cut in undifferentiated strata, divided by islands and branching into tributary bays. Into one of these we drifted more by the virtue of the tide than of any wind as the moon chased the last light of the sun out of the sky, and into the silence of that black pool surrounded by black mountains let go the anchor.

The morning sun gradually dispersed a fog which had gathered during the night and showed opposite us on the beach a colossal anchor carved in stone, a record of the fact that this was Captain Cook's first landing-place. It was a good spot to choose; the hills behind it, as far as the eye could reach, were thickly wooded; opposite it the bright coloured rocks of Motuara and Long Island distracted the eye from the barren ridges on the other side of the sound. As we proceeded we opened up larger and more beautiful bays than Ship Cove, where we had anchored. But there was something very obviously wrong with the look of the country. It was the fire, as against the axe. One saw either unlimited virgin forest (which is very monotonous) or a desolation. You cannot save from the burning a grove of fine trees to shelter and beautify your future farm, and the planted trees are of course still negligible. And that is why Picton, or any other place in New Zealand, is quite unlike Glengariff.

I did not see anything of New Zealand at this time, for I was confined to Picton by a strike on the railways; which in a way was rather a convenience, for I was able to get my mainsail mended by a sailmaker who would otherwise have been making tarpaulins for goods wagons. Indeed at any time I hardly saw more than the townspeople, and the soul of no country dwells in its cities. I regretted this, for it struck me as being a most interesting country in a curious stage of development. Apart from the considerable section of the commercial classes which is badly Americanized one gets the impression of an intense Nationalism—in some cases of Nationalism run mad, which accounts for a good deal of the jealousy of strangers and intolerance of foreign ideas sometimes shown—and of the Nation becoming less and less the Dominion of New Zealand and more and more Maoriland. There is the spectacle, perhaps unique, of two races living on equal terms, but still apart; and of the colonists carefully guarding the language and traditions of the natives. The average New Zealander's knowledge of his country would put to shame the average Irishman. If he could isolate his country till the rawness had worn off he would develop a culture certainly singular and possibly very fine; unfortunately the seeds of corruption come in every week from Sydney, Vancouver, or San Francisco.

I have no right to make these speculations, for I am not a journalist but only a master mariner. However, in this latter capacity I have a right to grumble at the organization for providing me with Greenwich time. After many fruitless attempts to get a time signal from Wellington I had to search for a man who had a receiving-set that would hear San Francisco; and thus I rated my chronometer, completed with stores and water, collected my crew, and on May 1st sailed for Montevideo and Dublin.

We got a famous shove off, with a fresh breeze of wind and clear weather, and next morning took leave of New

Zealand when a cloud shadow swept the rosy brilliance of the snow slopes on the huge ridges of the Kaikoura Mountains, 9,000 feet high and 70 or 80 miles astern, into invisibility. But we were not destined to get far. The wind became southerly and the sea rough, and I ran away to the northward to look for better conditions; then on the third night out, W., the mate, slipped on the wet deck and hit his knee against a belaying-pin. We kept on sailing at a great pace, and I did not mind getting rather too far North and making sure of going well clear of the Chatham Islands; but when it came on to blow a south-easterly gale with a very high sea it looked as if my efforts might rather be wanted to keep clear of New Zealand; so I hove-to and investigated W.'s leg. He had dismissed the injury rather lightly at first, but now it was badly swollen, and I made him lie up. There was nothing to do anyway except to keep ourselves warm and dry till the wind shifted. Meanwhile the yacht, under reefed staysail sheeted a little to windward of the mast, and double-reefed mainsail, was lying pretty comfortably about five points off the wind, making two or two and a half knots through the water and as many points of leeway. At four o'clock next morning, however, either she paid off too much or an exceptional sea came up abeam; anyway it broke more or less all over her. Exactly how much I do not know, we were all turned in at the time; it threw G. out of his bunk and woke me to find the cabin in darkness and full of the noise of rushing waters—but it is surprising what a lot of noise a very little water makes. I jumped for the gas and lit it. Blessed is acetylene as an illuminant for small yachts. Had that been an electric bulb it would certainly have been broken. I saw then that the small quantity of water had put the ship in imminent danger. It was lying, some 9 inches deep, against the locker in which all our matches were stored—in paper parcels, if you can believe the incredible folly of it! We splashed down to leeward and threw them out before the water had time to filter through. I never saw G. move so quickly before or since. The casualties were negligible, but I had learned another lesson in caution and in the use of tin boxes. The only casualty on deck was a sack of coal washed over the side.

This was the only heavy water the ship ever took, and it was unfortunate that I did not see how she took it, or why. Possibly I was carrying too much sail, or head-reaching too quickly, but I did not want to drift dead to leeward as long as I could make some progress more or less in the right direction; otherwise it would have been a case for oil-bags and a sea-anchor. There was a third reef band in the mainsail, and I suppose that a prudent mariner would have had that tied down; but neither at this nor at any other time was it used. I have not of course any idea of the form or size of that sea; I expect it differed from the others more in its direction than in its magnitude. It did not heave us over very far, which was reassuring, for I was much more afraid of being rolled right over by a bad sea than of having decks and skylights broken in and being swamped; at the worst it was only a ducking, and one cannot expect to get round the world without that.

We were now about 200 miles north of the Chatham Islands and W.'s knee was so bad that somebody had to stick a knife into it. I was very glad when he said, "I'm an older Captain than you, and have opened dozens of them," and did it himself. But I did not care for a six weeks' voyage with a man who had a septic wound, for there was nothing ahead of us nearer than Punta Arenas, so I decided to run back for New Zealand as soon as the sea moderated. I wasted a day, for after the scare of the previous night I was afraid of being swamped when the ship started sailing, before she brought the wind right aft. I did not realize that a small vessel is perfectly safe, however she lies with regard to the wind, as long as she has no way on her; and that *Saoirse* in particular, canvassed as she was, would pay off instantaneously as soon as she gathered way. It was a bad mistake, for once the wind started to drop it would drop away altogether, and an easterly wind in these parts is a valuable rarity. But in spite of the inevitable westerly which followed, we got to Napier in Hawkes Bay on the 10th of May.

During the ten days I spent in Napier there were two gales, one heavy flood, and I saw three houses falling down the hill-side into the main street. A few days after I left it was worse; the harbour feil out into the bay; and they were lucky to salve the lighthouse, which floated— so the Harbour Engineer told me: but he is an Englishman, and may be prejudiced. Anyway it appears to be a pretty tough place for weather. Between gales it froze, the alleviation to which was that I got frost-fish, and they are very good to eat. They say that these fish, when it freezes, come up out of the sea and lie on the beaches, so that when they are stiff the people come and take them away to the refrigerators, for they are very delicate and would not otherwise bear the handling: but I would suggest that they are so called rather because when they come on shore the beach appears to be covered by a thin sheet of ice from under which the water has run away, leaving it white and uneven of surface, so silvery are they. I do not know anything in Nature that looks quite so unsubstantial as a frost-fish.

Besides the Englishman I found a friend in the office of the Steam Trawling Company, who gave me two much-needed charts of the coast and of the approaches to Auckland. For W. was going to be a month in hospital, and I was quite sure that Providence, having turned me back in the month of May, was not going to let me start for the Horn late in June. I had two alternatives before me: to sell my yacht or to find some one who would contribute to the expenses of a cruise round the Islands till it was the season for the Southern Ocean; for either, I must go to Auckland, and there I went with G., leaving W. to follow.

The passage was uneventful, so I will enliven it with another albatross story. We were running with a fresh following breeze across the Bay of Plenty with a fishing line out astern, the bait just skipping along the surface of the water. The albatross interested himself in it, and of course tried to come at it in the orthodox way, dropping into the water head to wind; and naturally he could not turn quick enough to catch it. I substituted a hookless bait, for I did not want any more of the weather we had in the Tasman Sea, and called G. to look at the fun. The bird tried again two or three times in the same way, once indeed nearly catching the bait, which was a stout piece of rag, but in such an awkward position that he would have got a fine ducking if he had succeeded. He swore gently to himself, got up, and took a turn or two round the ship, thinking. Then he came at it straight down wind. That looked even more hopeless, for if we were doing 7 knots the wind was doing 20, and the bird must have been doing something more than that. However, he hit the back of a wave and drove along in a smother of foam, scrambling with his feet to try to get a hold on the water, the tips of his half-closed wings just touching the surface to balance him. At last he stood upright, planing along on his feet with his toes well turned up and his back feathers blowing over his head; a ridiculous enough sight, but coming up on that bait like a bonito. I will not swear that he did not wink an eye at us, as if to say, "Now, you overgrown penguins that thought you could play a trick on me, look!" and we did look, while very carefully he stretched his neck out over the bait, and very gingerly he bent his beak down towards it. But whether it was because he lowered his toes in sympathy with his eyes, or because his balance shifted with his gaze, he tripped, turned a complete somersault, and came up spluttering and sneezing to find us in fits of laughter. He jumped into the air with the most horrible language and went off at his best speed to Bounty Island where there is only the kind of penguin that dare not play practical jokes on an albatross.

Of course I had to see the local volcano as I passed, but it was a poor thing, a little rubbish-heap of an island with a wisp of steam upon one side of it; and at night quite invisible. As a matter of fact that night one could not see distant objects, we were so blinded by the light our own passage made in the water. My dingy old mainsail was so brilliantly lit by the wave under the lee bow that it showed pale against the sky—rather an unearthly sight—and from our stern a long luminous furrow extended like a comet's tail into infinity, which gave an illusion of speed that the patent log quite failed to confirm. It is curious that I never noticed any quantity of general phosphorescence in the water except near the land, and in one case off the African coast, where the appearance of the sea next morning suggested that a submarine volcano had shifted some of the land near us. But of localized phosphorescence I saw a remarkable example in the Tasman Sea; great lumps of light like grossly obese sausages a foot or more in length, and probably colonies of Pyrosoma.

The next day we sailed between noble mountains and beautifully wooded islands of every shape and size, not mere pieces of rock covered with scrub, but parklands of the greenest grass varied by fine groves of trees. I had not seen grass since leaving Ireland, and the Tamaki Strait reminded me a good deal of the Shannon below Foynes; and I wished it were really the Shannon, for I was very tired of the whole voyage and of perpetually engaging and discharging men, and of the fearful expense which such an operation involves in a country where seamen's wages are £15 per month; and I was very near running my ship on a rock in the fog this morning, only the sea was rather rough and my boat was fairly rotten and G. was very heavy and I was afraid we might get drowned. But when I saw the magnificent scenery and the hundreds of sheltered harbours of the Hauraki Gulf and thought of the thousands of yachtsmen in Auckland I was glad that I had not wrecked my yacht, for I could surely sell her. Or, since it was now winter, many of the local yachts would be laid up and I should easily get a crew for a Polynesian trip. So at noon on a Sunday I let go my anchor near the yacht moorings in Auckland Harbour, and waited for visitors.

A reporter of the morning paper came. I told him first

and foremost, and plain and clear (for Australian reporters are marvels at getting a story wrong), two things. First, that I was in a bad and temporary anchorage, and would the Harbour Master put me into a proper one; and second, that my ensign was that of the Club that gives one the best dinner in Dublin, and if the Secretary of the Squadron would introduce me to possible purchasers or possible crews I would do so much and more for any New Zealander that happened to visit Dunleary. I do not know what printer's devil got hold of my story, for I did not see next morning's paper; it blew a gale that night, and after dragging my anchor all over Stanley Bay I found myself right in the fairway of the ferry-boats, with my dinghy swamped and the oars lost. So I spent most of that day making a pair of oars out of various scraps of timber and repairing the boat; but nobody came to order me out of a very inconvenient anchorage. The next day was foggy; I hailed a ferry-boat that was feeling her way past and asked the Captain to send some one to shift me; but he said, "Not while this fog lasts; your bell is such a splendid guide to help us to find the pier."

On the third day, the fog having cleared and my boat being mended, I found the Harbour Master and got a berth alongside the quays, and then discovered, I think, the reason why I was getting rather a cool reception. Either that reporter was phenomenally stupid, or some other intelligent person had seen the Harp in the fly of my Ensign, but failed to see the Crown or the Union; anyhow the report was put about that I was flying the flag of the Irish Republic. The New Zealanders are very strong at waving Union Jacks (as they call any kind of flag), but are rather weak at distinguishing them.

While I was at Picton there was a regatta on, for which of course my ship was properly dressed, and a rather muzzy old gentleman came along wanting to know why I did not haul that Union Jack down. I could not imagine what he objected to in my old Red Ensign, into which I had with great labour sewed four stars for the honour of New Zealand—and if there is a crabbeder job than sewing bunting I don't know it. Eventually I found out that he was referring to the tricolour of the Irish Free State! And on another occasion when I was flying the plain, undefaced Blue Ensign another old gentleman gravely lectured me for appropriating the flag of the Royal New Zealand Yacht Squadron. It was rather hard sometimes to know what to do; but the more serious misunderstandings were soon cleared up, and the people of the port hastened to make handsome amends.

I had now to pay off G., which I did with regret, but I could not let a wages bill run on while I did not know what was going to happen to the ship. I could not sell her; the Auckland yachtsmen have their playground so close at hand that they do not want a sea-going type of boat. My other idea, of going round the Tonga, Samoa, and Fiji Islands, was by no means a new one; everybody asked me why I did not go, till I retorted by asking why they did not come; and then followed a great silence. If I ever hoped to bring my boat home I should have to wait till W. came back before I went yachting anywhere, as I wanted to keep hold of him at least as a nucleus of a crew.

But when he did come back he was in a very unsettled frame of mind, and it was disconcerting and painful to me to see the change in my previously charming companion. It would require a better psychologist than I to deal with his moods, and a more tactful pen than mine to describe them. Fortunately he was entertained a good deal by old friends who were eminently respectable, for he was drifting away from me. I thought that a couple of weeks at sea and new countries would bring him back to his old self, but I did not feel like risking even the short passage to the Tonga Islands with him alone, and continued to look for the passenger. I refused the first one that offered, for which I was sorry afterwards, for she would have pulled W. together; but she wanted to go to the Solomon Islands, and I had heard that if one was not eaten there one died of horrible diseases; besides, I had an obsession about the Trade Wind, and did not want to go so far West. Eventually I did get a passenger, and I did get to Tonga; but I got no farther, and I came back much sooner than I had intended with yet another new crew, natives of the Islands.

One of the Tonga boys left me, and while I was looking for a substitute I had an opportunity of seeing a little of Auckland, though I never got outside the town, because I had no safe place to leave the ship. I should have hauled her out of the water on a pretext of repairs to the hull and left her up on the beach, but only the Harbour Board's slip was available, and that was impossibly expensive. As it was, I was generally lying alongside a quay or, more comfortably, another vessel, but always on the look-out for a northerly wind. If it came by day, I got towed off to an anchorage on the other side of the harbour. This was not satisfactory, because by now I had no boat, and it appears to be impossible to beg, borrow or hire a boat in Auckland.

Once indeed I succeeded in hiring a boat; the owner
wanted ten shillings a day for her and wanted it in advance, as she leaked so badly that we might not be able
to bring her back. The Power Boat Club indeed would
have helped me in the matter of communications if I
had been able to get moorings anywhere near their
house, but I could not. If the wind came at night, I
could only make fenders. For the benefit of others who
may be in the same predicament, I will give away the
secret of making fenders. You steal two coal-baskets,
knock the bottom out of one, slit it up the side, roll it up
and shove it in the other; if the baskets are rather old
and worn you will be able to get the bottom in, too; if
not, your fender is of exactly the right consistency for a
boat of 30 tons or so and lasts a surprisingly long time.

Auckland, because it has more natural advantages,
has thrown away more architectural opportunities than
any other city that I know. There are some fine buildings in it, but they are always spoiled somehow, as the
new shed on the Princes Wharf, the best thing of its
kind, is spoiled by an ugly little weighbridge house stuck
down opposite the principle façade. And there are some
interesting buildings. From across the harbour I was
struck by the beauty of the block of flats in Shortland
Street; on investigation they proved to be a fine example of the Auckland ferro-concrete Gothic, a very
dignified style if not so amusing as the Morocco-rococo
Gothic of St. Vincent in the Cape Verde Islands. In the
new University Buildings it becomes positively flam-
boyant, a daring if not quite successful experiment; at
any rate it shows that the Auckland architects are not
mere copyists; they are evolving a treatment of ferro-
concrete construction based on timber design, which

is both good history (for the Stone Age hardly existed here) and good Art. But why do they not get the City Council to regulate planning, and prevent the finest site in the town from being littered indiscriminately with hideous cubes of glass and concrete instead of being laid out with beautiful terraced gardens and houses of a fabulous rental? Eighty years ago Auckland did not exist; now it has all the problems of traffic and space that vex cities ten times as old. Fortunately New Zealand is liable to earthquakes.

Meanwhile I was having a terrible time in my search for a crew. A discharge on a loose sheet of paper, as is the rule here, either is "very good" or is torn up; and no more helpful are recommendations from people who know nothing about the men they are introducing. In one case an applicant for the job of mate was far better known to the police, a fact that I learned too late to save my purse. It was more serious that I might not have found out his ability till it was too late to save my ship.

With the material available it was unlikely that I should find anyone sufficiently competent and enthusiastic to stand watch and watch with me if we had heavy weather going round the Horn (for all my friends said that K., the Tongan, would die long before I got there), so I resigned myself to looking for two more or less competent slaves. I interviewed a long procession of incompetents who merely wanted to get home, but I had to tell them that it was no good to me to save on wages if I lost my life. (They evidently estimated their own lives at their true value.) At last two Irishmen came along with sailing-ship discharges; and that was the end of my stay in New Zealand.

CHAPTER VII

TONGA

ONE could not decently visit the South Pacific without seeing something of the South Pacific Islands. My intention had been to go first to the Tonga group, then perhaps to Samoa, but anyway to Fiji before returning to Auckland. I anticipated an extremely soft job as far as sailorizing went, for I should be in the Trade Wind Zone most of the time, and this was not the season of hurricanes; accordingly I sent all my good sails ashore to be overhauled and repaired, leaving myself with some old rags which were condemned long since and which I thought had finished their service when they brought me down from Madeira to Pernambuco. I also cleared out everything else that was not actually in use; sea-anchor, storm-oil, spare spars, water-breakers, and a couple of coils of rope, which left no loose gear on deck except the boat; and the resulting space and freedom were very comfortable on the outward passage and still more so on my return, when the boat also had disappeared. I rather overlooked, however, the fact that I had 800 miles of southern winter seas to cross before I reached the Tropic of Capricorn, and I did not know that this particular bit of sea had an unenviable reputation for roughness.

When one is going yachting, as I was now, one ought to have no preconceived plans, but just make a fair wind of everything, and since a clearance is necessary for a foreign voyage, get that clearance made out for some port on the other side of the world, so that whatever place one descends on is on the way to one's destination, in case Customs officials ask what one is doing there. But I thought it was time to show the world that I could actually get to the place I said I was going to (a thing which had not happened to me during the past year) and therefore got a clearance for Nukualofa in Tonga-tabu. Nothing is hid from the postal officials of a small town, and next day the published mail notice advertised that the *Saoirse* was taking the Tonga mail on the following day. I thought it could not amount to much, because the regular mail steamer had sailed only three days before, but when it came down in a huge red motor lorry I was very glad that I had made a clearance in the sail-room. Being committed in respect of the mail I could hardly refuse a modest amount of cargo, though it had to be put on board surreptitiously as I had cleared in ballast. Last of all a pigeon enthusiast embarked three birds which I was instructed to let go at distances of one, two, and three hundred miles from the land. It appeared to me to be asking rather a lot of the third, for the weather did not look very encouraging for flying pigeons, or, for the matter of that, for yachting. Indeed, but for the mail, I do not know when I should have got off, for I am a singularly bad starter, but it included a portentous Consular bag marked "Urgent"; so, having received half-a-crown from the Post Office and five shillings for freight on my cargo, I expended the sum on the hire of a motor-launch to pull me away from the wharf. This was a necessity, for the wind was right on shore and I was hemmed in on one side by a pile-driver and on the other by a movie-ship (I presume that describes the s.s. *Hollywood* of Los Angeles), so I do not feel that I prejudiced the status of *Saoirse* as a yacht or of myself as an amateur yachtsman.

I always discount the happenings of the first day or two at sea, especially if there is a head wind and dirty weather, as on this occasion, and do not try to size up my crew until they have recovered from their sea-sickness. I therefore assumed that all was well, and sent a message by the first pigeon asking that our mail should be sent to Suva, as we should have left Tonga before the next boat arrived. Then the wind hauled aft, C., the passenger, came to life, and I entrusted him with the wheel for a few minutes that night. It was certainly dark, and a little squally, but that was no reason why he should have turned the ship right round and got her taken aback. This is an operation which I do not encourage at all; at the best it means considerable delay and hard work, for one has to take the foresail in before one can get the ship under command; this night it nearly lost me the foresail, for the tack carried away, and the flogging sail made a nasty obstacle to dodge in order to get at the brails, which led forward of all and were made fast on the forestay. I did not get much help from the others while I was muzzling that sail—nor after I had made it fast. I expected none from C., and W. had gone on strike, so I kept under easy canvas during the night, and in the morning sent off the two remaining pigeons with a message cancelling that of the previous day and saying that I should return direct from Tonga as soon as possible. Had it not been for the mail I believe I should have turned back then and there, for I could see plenty of trouble ahead.

The unfortunate pigeons, however, were in more immediate trouble. I was very sorry for them, for I could not bring myself to look upon them as merely a substitute for a wireless installation; if one cannot reach the land with wireless no one is the worse, if one fails to reach it with a pigeon it is the pigeon's funeral. I was only about 200 miles distant equally from Cape Brett and from the Barriers, but it was a dull morning with a fresh breeze blowing from that direction. I understand that a pigeon just flies round in circles till it sees its home; if so, as the visibility was poor and they would be continually drifting off shore, they would have to fly thousands of miles before they saw anything except the Kermadec Islands, which were rather farther off, but to leeward. Anyway they never got back to Auckland; at the time it was blowing a south-westerly gale on the coast.

I had no more than a fresh breeze, but there was a rough sea, and the steering gear began to give trouble, so I hove-to in order to remedy it. As the ship rounded up into the wind, the pin of a shackle in the jib-sheet broke, and that ancient sail vanished with hardly a sound. Never use small galvanized ironwork; better to rust your sails than to lose them. The only substitute I had on board was a very light and very rotten flying-jib, and I was not going to risk that except in very light winds. Anyway I was not going to bend it that day; I had a heaven-sent opportunity for a long night in bed and I took it, for I was not quite certain how things were going to be worked for the next week.

I had of course to make what use I prudently could of my crew; it cost me a broken skylight, very nearly lost my gaff-topsail, and, most unpardonable crime of all, was the cause of a huge rent in my very shaky old mainsail; for one can get somewhere without jibs or gaff-topsails, but if that mainsail had gone to pieces we should have been indeed helpless.

However, in spite of my solicitude about the flying-jib, which made me haul it down at every puff of wind, and often take in the mizzen as well to balance the ship; in spite of days of light baffling airs and calms, and an almost uninterruptedly abominable sea, I crawled along slowly to the northward, and at last got light Trade Winds that put the sails asleep in the smooth water, and we began to slip along swiftly and quietly in a silence that was startling after the banging of sheets, the creaking of spars and blocks, and the clash of sliding crockery; but by then the voyage was almost ended, and next evening I went up on to the foreyard to see for the first time a coral island.

Eua is indeed not a coral island, except in the sense that it is an island made of coral rock, for it has stopped growing, and instead of lying flush with the water is hove up a thousand feet into the air. Providence did well for the mariner in planting at the two ends of the Tonga group the lofty beacons of Eua and Vavau, as a warning against the low islets and reefs that lie all between. Just before dark I saw its dim shape some 30 miles away, and stood off and on for daylight and a fair ride to enter the narrow channel into Nukualofa Harbour.

Eua Island seen close to under a brilliant sun is a wonderful sight, but rather too green and luscious for my own taste. Even here in the Tropics it seems incredible that such heavy-foliaged trees should grow right down the cliffs, where one might suppose they would have been uprooted or broken by the wind and blasted by the spray; they grow so thickly that they are monotonous and one is grateful for any accident that exposes a patch of the creamy rock. This morning it was the colour of the sea that was really beautiful. I was gradually shoaling the water over a bottom of white coral sand which lightened its tint to a heavenly blue, and on this the freshening breeze had raised white horses that were racing towards a row of bushy heads of palms, the trunks of which were sunk below the horizon. But as I approached they climbed out of the water, aided no doubt to some extent by a mirage, and grew to a fabulous height above a strip of dazzling beach which was interrupted from time to time by the still whiter foam of the breakers on the reef.

I pricked off my position in the entrance of the channel by bearings taken with a doubtful compass of islands which I could not identify with any certainty, and steered up it between the reefs which gradually closed in on either hand. It was unnecessary to complicate my navigation by inaccurate observations; I had got into the region of coral pilotage, which, on a bright fine day like this with the light behind one, is far easier and more certain, even in a well-charted group like the Tonga Islands. The fairway of the channel was of the same brilliant azure as the water outside; not until one got into less than ten fathoms did it seem perceptibly lighter in colour. The edge of the reef was marked by a strong band of purple brown, comparatively narrow, as it appeared from my point of view; and beyond this, as far as I could see, in towards the land on the port side and a maze of small islands on the starboard, stretched the palest emerald tint over the dead reef which was forming an incipient miniature lagoon. I did not then have time to study these things in detail, for a boiling tide was pouring us through a narrow tortuous pass into the still waters of Nukualofa Harbour. And this is one of the places which one wants to enter with all one's sails set and drawing properly, for after Sydney it is probably the most critical of fore-and-aft seamanship in the South Pacific. Not in vain did I haul on halliards and sheets, and hoist the Tongan flag at the masthead, and the Quarantine flag at the starboard yardarm and the Mail flag at the port and my own Tricolour abaft all, for I was expected on this day. (The Auckland postmaster must have been a pessimist, for he could not have known how my crew were going to turn out; I expected to, and I should in happier circumstances, have arrived two, or possibly three, days earlier.)

There is something to be said for running to scheduled places and times. Knowing that this was my destination I was able to buy that Tongan flag in Auckland, and that made me popular; I was able to bring the mail, and that made me more popular. And I had a tolerably smart yacht, which, if I had been willing to sell her, would have culminated my popularity, for a time at least. I was in fact offered a great deal more than the last European yacht that came out here fetched, though she was a much bigger boat; but I was not selling. For *Saoirse*, being built with iron fastenings, could not be sheathed with copper on account of galvanic action, and unsheathed she wanted regular docking and painting to keep out worms; which could not be done in these islands where the range of tide is small and there are no slipways.

I let W. and C. have the boat to go ashore straight away and look for lodgings in the town, telling them to send her back for me in the cool of the evening when I might be expected to make my number at the Nuku-alofa Club. They failed to do so, but I did not much mind; I was rather tired anyway, so I dined, largely on fruit thrown on board from a passing cutter, and turned in. But next morning I had to take the ship's articles to the Consulate and the particulars of my jib to the sail-maker.

I had anchored rather far out; remembering previous experiences in Port Said and St. Vincent I wanted to be beyond the radius of action of flies; an unnecessary pre-caution here, for there are no flies on Tongatabu, unless you count mosquitoes, and a very short space of salt water will stop them. I was so far out that when the Trade Wind was blowing up to average I could not hail the jetty, but that was immaterial. I had hardly run up the appropriate flag signal when the Queen's Har-bour Master sent off a boat and two men for my use as long as I stayed in the port, for my late crew had left my boat bumping on the reef all night and she was not worth salving. A good riddance anyway, for she was only a folding canvas contraption, as long as I was in the Friendly Islands; indeed Auckland was the only place where I had any need of a boat of my own.

I paid W. off at the Consulate, and I found the sail-maker making a clock (he also makes pianos and all kinds of music) and ordered a new jib. Then there did not seem to be any reason why I should not enjoy my-self by doing nothing until the danger of worms made it desirable for me to go back to Auckland and dock the ship. I did this very thoroughly; I did not even go as far as Vavau, which was rather unenterprising, seeing that I could almost certainly have paid my expenses by carrying passengers. That would have been perhaps hardly fair on the local boats, but it would have been in the interests of the travelling public; for I never saw anything so disgracefully overcrowded as those local boats. However, I stayed all my fortnight in Nukualofa, examining those things which were very near to me, and for everything else taking the word of the local historian. The nearest thing of all was a little patch called Monu, a cable's length from my anchorage, a miniature model of a coral island; and that set me examining the structure and growth of coral islands generally and of Tongatabu in particular.

The history of most atolls in this group is quite simple, and I will construct one without calling on Darwin's theory of subsidence. It started with a volcano; there are plenty of them hereabouts from time to time, but the local variety is short-lived. Falcon Island, for instance, was three miles long and 160 feet high and in four years had been washed right away. However, when it has so far washed away that there is sixty fathoms of water over it, it goes no farther, for wave action ceases at that depth. And just at that depth the work of the coral insect begins. He is a very much better builder than the volcano, and once he has laid a bed of concrete over the loose scoria his work is permanent and limited only by the level of low water. It is difficult to study his habits on the outer reef, on account of the surf, but here, in Nukualofa Harbour, which is itself a big lagoon, the shoal patches are becoming miniature atolls. Naturally the coral does not grow so luxuriantly as in the open ocean, but one can see it safely at one's leisure as one drifts over it in a small boat on the glassy water.

That is an amazing sensation, and it is hard to realize that one is not suspended over a steep sandy cliff, crowned with a thicket of furze-bushes. It is almost impossible to believe that these are not vegetable growths; I shall call them without apology by the names of the plants they resemble, it being understood always that everything is coral, and, moreover, in the way of colour would eclipse our most fiery autumn hill-side.

At the bottom of the steep slope of sand, where the blue of deep water changes to green, are tall clumps of broom; they are growing on fragments of solid rock which have fallen down from the overhanging verge of the cliff, and in the still water throw out their long, straight, slender spikes, dotted with crimson flowers, to a far greater distance than those nearer the surface. As the ground rises rapidly under us the growths become more bushy and stand closer together, and the brilliancy of their colours is no longer modified by the medium, now colourless, through which they are seen. Then all at once the cliff is hidden by the fringe of what might be furze, but each branch is tipped with blue instead of with gold. How far the solid rock is below us we cannot tell, nothing can be seen through the dense tangle. Here the tops of the plants are neatly levelled off; that patch of bright green, like a big club-moss, shows stalks all the same length; the creeping juniper sends no errant twigs above the line of low water. But here and there are depressions in the close-cropped bank, where grow the pale leaves of a monstrous bog-violet, a saucer-shaped fungus, brown and purple, or the white hemispheres of mushrooms.

But not a tithe of the colour that delights us is in the coral or in any thing of jelly, sessile or crawling. Brighter than any butterfly, flashing more changeably than any humming-bird, are the little burnished fishes, that hover over and dart between the branches; some of gold, some of copper, some of emerald banded with deepest ultramarine, and some of the most marvellous blue that exists in the world, and all with iridescent lights and waves of other colours playing over them as they swim. One can hardly allot a definite tint to anything about a living coral reef; the dullest browns and purples, which seem most prevalent, with a changing ray of the sun are shot with green and violet.

A little farther in, where the furze-bushes have died and their stripped stalks are falling into decay, patches of rock or sand show between the mosses; and here we can see the things that creep along the bottom; fantastic sea-urchins and starfishes, crabs and sea-slugs, coming shyly out of their holes, for the slabs of rock that look so solid are but the tangled branches of the coral cemented together, and there is a whole underground life in the cavities beneath them. And woebetide the wanderers if they walk into the wrong hole, for it may be the gaping mouth of a giant clam that would take a man's foot off.

Towards the centre of our immature atoll the coral has been broken up or dissolved away and reconsolidated as a rock floor, which has sunk in the process; sand is accumulating in the hollows; it is an embryo lagoon. Meanwhile blocks of stone have been thrown up on the edge of the reef; and are now dry at half tide. In time they will accumulate above high-water; some day a cocoanut will drift ashore and strike root, and behold the finished article! Thus, like a fairy ring, the coral island is always growing outwards and dying in the middle, and in many cases it requires nothing more catastrophic than a sixty-fathom bank to start it. But to finish such an island as Tongatabu or Vavau requires not only immense time but a Darwinian subsidence; we can see that the rock is a thousand feet thick, and we do not know how much there is under or how much there once was on top of that thousand feet.

After the coral reefs the most distinctive thing about these islands is the cocoanut palm, and it is far more conspicuous and insistent. In its first quality it is a blessing to the mariner, who welcomes the day when the first palm grove marks a hitherto invisible reef; in its second, which attacks the sense of smell, no doubt it is all right for those who are accustomed to it, but not for me. The landing stairs on the jetty at Nukualofa do not go down quite far enough to meet a small boat at a low spring-tide, and something of a scramble is required to get ashore; and since bags of copra are landed in the same place it is all smeared with palm oil and extremely detrimental to one's clothes, unless one is both discreet and agile in one's scrambling. And Tonga is one of those over-civilized countries which pay great attention to clothes, and has enacted laws defining the minima. I was glad to see, however, that the people no longer wear a suit of pilot-cloth on Sundays as described by Frank Bullen. What a depressing and dirty-looking thing is a crowd in Europe compared with one in Brazil or these Islands! I do not know who does the washing, or who pays for the soap in these places, but laundering must be an immense industry. When I was at Auckland some Fijians brought a coal hulk down from Suva into the next berth; I never saw them except looking freshly washed and starched and ironed all over. I had to buy a suit of ready-made clothes in the nearest shop before I ventured ashore in the daytime at Nukualofa.

The first thing I saw delighted me very much, though at first it made me think I was dreaming. It would not have been out of place in one of those remote villages in the French Jura where the seventeenth-century architect of the Town Hall still leaned heavily on the Romanesque, but as Government offices in the South Pacific it was almost incredible. With the exception of the Post Office it is the only stone building in the place, and it was never copied, for the rain pours through the soft coral rock. I heard that it was built by a French missionary, and it was a very pleasant link with home to think of that Frenchman reproducing, as well as he could remember it, some building out of his own parish fourteen thousand miles away. Or that other person who made the beautiful inscription on a certain concrete rain-water tank which, as far as the lettering goes (for it is the Tongan language), might have been cut on a well-head in North Italy. For good or ill Tonga has adopted a European civilization, and many of the posts in the Government are occupied by real Englishmen, Irishmen, and Scotsmen who are helping to keep the country from lapsing into barbarism. The one deplorable thing, the thing which the visitor is bound to notice first, is that all the larger buildings in the town look as if they had been imported ready-made from Auckland. Auckland, alas, is fourteen times as near as Europe.

There are still, however, a good many houses in the old tradition, which is a curious one; indeed I saw one of them under construction. It was walled with reeds stuck into the ground, a dozen of them inclined to the right, a dozen to the left, and so on; so that by interlacing them a firm surface was obtained. Evidently one cannot work round corners with this system, so there are no corners; the house has an apse at either end, which presents no difficulties for a thatched roof. But suitable reeds are becoming scarce, and weather-boarding is found to be more durable. The only differ-ence this makes to the plan is that the apses are five-sided instead of semicircular on plan. This must involve a tedious amount of fitting of short ends of boarding, and one wonders why a race of shipwrights do not bend the planks round the curve, but they do not. And when it comes to shaping a corrugated iron roof to fit the building, as is the fashion these days, I should, for all my prejudices, chuck tradition and make my house rectangular. They say that the rounded ends are more resistant to hurricanes; but not many hurricanes came to Nukualofa, and there are plenty of square houses which have not been blown down by them. The Ton-gan's prejudices, though, are stronger than mine, and however square his house may be by first intention he generally contrives to cut a corner off it somewhere. He builds his churches also with an apse at either end, but how much this is, like the Government building, a leaning on the Romanesque I do not know. They are enormous and innumerable, every sect seems to have two or three in this town alone; but there are no other concert halls, and pictures only twice a week.

All these houses are set in a veritable garden, and each one of them stands in the middle of a beautifully kept lawn of fine short grass—each householder has to sweep it daily, under penalty. There are plenty of hand-some trees everywhere (I cannot include the cocoanut palm under this designation), but not so closely planted as to make the turf under them coarse or patchy. They are, however, rather disappointing in the way of height;

the tallest are the grove of Norfolk Island pines planted round the Palace by the late King; in time they will grow to 150 or 200 feet. Not only is there grass all round the houses, but some of the side streets are of grass. It seems incredible that in a country with an annual rainfall of 60 inches they should not be morasses, but the subsoil is very porous, and so they keep in wonderfully good order. But where the traffic is heavy Tonga is in the same trouble as the rest of the world; the soft coral limestone will not stand fast motor lorries.

The extraordinary neatness and tidiness of the whole town was the more surprising when I saw the enormous number of pigs in the place; but perhaps the Tongan pig has been trained to look for his food elsewhere than in one's front garden; and of fowls, which are the next creatures after pigs for messing things up. The most conspicuous livestock was horses; no Tongan ever walks, and most of them cannot afford motor-cars, whose range of action is limited in any case by the indifferent nature of the roads. All these animals do not prevent flowers from growing luxuriantly everywhere; why should I moan about the horrid architecture when most of it is discreetly hidden? And over the flowers large and brilliant butterflies, which, as there is not a butterfly net on the island, hover round one so closely as to seem larger and more brilliant than Nature made them.

The generosity of the islanders is notorious. They have a good life themselves, and want every one else to share it; and why not? The kava bowl stands behind the door, pigs and yams grow quickly and cocoanuts are always falling from the trees; there are no congested districts, landless men, or unemployed. But their own idea of life is not to sit still all day and wait for yams and pigs to drop into their mouths. No Polynesian has quite got over the wandering instinct that sent him across thousands of miles of ocean to colonize these and other islands. The Tongans, I am told, had dreams comparatively recently of an overseas Empire, and started it by fitting out a fleet of great canoes each carrying a hundred men to conquer Fiji. It met with some success, though not with the complete submission of the country, and the Tongan colony remained autonomous and very powerful for a long time. An old Fijian told me that he would have preferred annexation by the Tongans, who regarded his people as Melanesians, rather than by the English, who regarded them as niggers; but Fijian politics are sadly complicated by the ubiquitous Indian problem. The Tongans were sufficiently proud of the outcome of this expedition to commemorate it with a sort of triumphal arch, a very handsome great trilithon. They still extend their conquests over Fiji, but in a more peaceful sphere; recently they gave that country a good beating at football. The Tongans consider themselves the most football-playing people in the world, and were talking of sending over a team to prove that claim as against New Zealand.

But no one now can travel for the sake of conquest, and only a few can travel for the sake of football; the rest travel for the sake of travel, and do so in anything that will float. I saw the Nomuka ferry-boat coming in one pretty breezy morning; she was a little cutter yacht, only half the size of mine, and had crossed sixty miles of open sea in that weather with nearly a score of passengers, men, women, and children, the latter packed into the dinghy so that they could not fall overboard. They had all spent the night on deck, for the hold was full of copra, and I suppose most of them had only come to pay a visit to their married sisters or to buy a yard of ribbon. And I might remark that the captains of these little craft do not shorten sail before it is necessary for the safety of the passengers, which means long after it is desirable for their comfort; for they are magnificent boatmen, as might be expected in a country composed entirely of small islands. And what material they have to work with! These swarms of tiny cutters are as likely as not outclassed racing yachts picked up cheap in Auckland; most unsuitable, one would think, but the people will not have a slow boat. That 35-ton yacht that was sold out here from Europe four years since is a thing of scorn and has been rechristened *The Milestone* in reference to her mobility.

Another day a smart-looking whaleboat came alongside having in her, in addition to the usual allowance of passengers and cargo, two harpoons, a lance, and two tubs of line—just on the chance that they might meet a whale (I wonder what would happen to the passengers and cargo if they did)—for this was the genuine article that fishes whales by hand in the primitive way, only she was put into trade just now, for it was not the season. I noticed in the Azores also that apart from the professional whalers, everybody went about armed with harpoons; I rather wondered, if one started throwing harpoons into sperm whales without having a proper boat or a proper crew to manage her, whose funeral it was going to be. I imagine that these two places must be about the last where the fishing is carried on in the old-fashioned way.

In such a country I could not fail to find good seamen, though they might not all be prepared to face the unknown and icy waters off the Horn; in fact so sure was I of not getting a bad seaman that I did not ask if applicants had any reason, other than a wanderlust, for wanting to leave their country.

K., who managed the principal garage in the town, had a regrettable accident with the best car. He said that his uncle was quite nice about it—K. is a bit of a spoiled child and will inherit all the old man's money —but I think the long-suffering uncle must have shown signs of turning. He has set K. up in various businesses to keep him out of mischief, but it is generally not long before he clears out to sea and is next heard of from Vancouver or Calcutta. I took on K., who is irresistible anyway, as soon as he applied.

B. was a rather bad bargain. I bailed him out of a mire of indebtedness in the hope that working under my eye he might be worth it to me; as he would have been if I had been assured of a continuous succession of hurricanes, earthquakes, and similar crises, for he was the best seaman I ever had on board; but in the lazy routine of fine weather I got no more out of him than his previous creditors had. I do not think he would have stood the cold farther south, and I was glad when he got a shore job in Auckland, where he had friends.

With this crew I was assured of a comfortable voyage back to New Zealand, for apart from their national passion for cleanliness they had been brought up to keep things tidy and make the best of life in small boats; moreover I found that K., as well as learning seamanship in small boats, had learned cookery on mail steamers, so at last I had someone who was certain to produce an equally good meal whether the ship was lying in harbour or butting into half a gale of wind.

When we sailed we were so loaded on deck with yams, bananas, oranges, green cocoanuts, and so forth that it was quite a job to find our flying-fish in the morning; and I might have filled the cabin with mats and rolls of tapa cloth had not my crew done so already. I may say that in the end they gave me a good half of the gear they brought on board, but then they indented rather heavily on me for clothes. B., who piloted me out, said that my boat, if not so handy as a cutter, was quite smart enough for the island trade, and that he was sorry I was not staying on as a business proposition; and indeed on that wonderful afternoon while we were racing along in the lee of that beautiful island, swinging slowly in the long perpetual swell, I felt sorry too; but it would not have done; I should have become lazier than suits my nature; one has to be born to this sort of thing.

For two days we had a fine breeze of wind and an average speed of $7\frac{1}{2}$ knots, and then got into the same area of calms and rough seas which had vexed me so much on the outward journey. But I was taking things more easily now. I had told the Postmaster that I was not going to kill myself getting the mails to Auckland at any particular time, and he said he didn't mind as long as I got there before the steamer did. So I nursed my shaky old mainsail very carefully, and on any excuse took it in. I had a brand-new jib and a brand-new storm mizzen, though it was a very little one, and my staysail was strong out of all proportion to its size; we achieved the acme of comfort under the two head-sails and that mizzen, and in spite of a really vicious assault on the part of the elements I was really far better off at sea than I should have been in Auckland.

But with all our dawdling, on the tenth day I saw the Little Barrier Island from the mast-head.

Now why, you ask, this place rather than the Bay of Islands? It seems the most inexcusable omission—apart from the fact that I should have landed the mails two days earlier—to have neglected to see this beautiful coast. I was not blown off it by westerly gales, I was not afraid of being blown on to it by easterly gales; it was just lack of enterprise only slightly palliated by the fact that I had no charts. After all my preaching about the virtue of seeing things with one's own eyes, there I was taking my Tongan history from the lips of K. and intending to take a description of the coast I was passing from a guide-book.

Next day we were in the neighbourhood of Little Barrier, and so long there that I was forced to make some observations on it. It is a curious lump of quite amorphous and quite rotten rock; it is just able to stand in vertical cliffs, but is so soft that every trickle of water cuts deep straight trenches in it; as far as I could see through the dense timber it must be a very exciting piece of sculpture, and I ought to have got there and seen how it was constructed. It is, however, a sanctuary for birds and beasts, and landing is prohibited. I suppose I could have got a permit, but again I felt unenterprising; I might even be called lazy.

On this occasion of my coming into Auckland I exercised the signal stations along the coast, always with the object of expediting the delivery of the mails, but perhaps also to avoid getting marooned again all Sunday waiting for pratique. They did not respond readily, but in the end the thing was done; the doctor was caught at the last moment, and while he was examining my bill of health his launch towed us up the harbour in a flat calm against a foul tide late on a Saturday evening (that was what I was thinking about when I hustled the signal stations so much) to our old berth ten days before the steamer came in with the pair who had left Auckland with me. And W., as I understand, married a wife who will make a much better hand of him than I did; and C. went, I hope, to the devil in his own way; and B. became a bricklayer's labourer, and I wonder if the bricklayer got any more work out of him than I did. But K. swore he would go on to the end of the world with me, and very notably did so.

CHAPTER VIII

CAPE HORN

THE serious nature of the business in which I had become involved is apparent from the title that I have put at the head of this chapter. So far I had not crossed the 40th parallel, but to get round the Horn I should have to go to 56° S.; so far I had only to deal with the ordinary easting weather, but in six weeks I should experience the intensified weather which haunts all great headlands, and in particular the greatest headland in the world. I had no doubt that sooner or later I should find myself in the Atlantic Ocean, unless indeed I tried imprudently to cut corners round the land, or came to grief in the Straits of Magellan, for I had only to keep the yacht afloat and sooner or later she would blow round; but we were now four of a ship's company, and taking into consideration the stores and water which could conveniently be carried I did not want to spend more than two months on the passage to Montevideo, for which port I had cleared. And to make an average speed of 5 knots over that distance would, I knew, mean either exceptional luck with the wind and sea, or a racing crew; and the latter was by far the more improbable thing of the two. K. I knew to be an average good small-boat sailor, but he had the misfortune to be an unusually good cook, so that his qualities as a seaman did not get full scope or their due appreciation; L. and M. were big-ship sailors, and that does not count for very much in these days when owners have cut down crews so much that captains cannot make passages.

In the forenoon of the 22nd of October I filled up with water and was ready for sea, and after luncheon I loosed the sails and prepared to get away. It was unfortunate that there were no seamen about, for the colonial longshoreman does not let go one's lines. The bight of my forward line rendered round the bollard all right, but the stern-line jammed behind a pile and I had to cut it. I had severed my last tie with New Zealand; I did not look back except to take my departure from East Cape two days later. "Taking a departure," in the language of the sea, is quite a different thing from cutting a mooring rope. Officially it is done thus: "East Cape bearing 285° distant 25 miles set course S. 76° E.," but it really means that you hope you will never see that country again, and, thank God, you can settle down to sea routine.

We were not the only things leaving the country that day, for here a tiny bird, very much like our gold-crested wren, was blown on board. We were then over 30 miles from the nearest land, and he could never have got home again in the prevailing westerly winds. At the time the wind was well to the southward, nearly on our beam, and in consequence there was a great back draught round the leach of the mainsail. Land birds, thinking that the spars and sails of a ship are parts of trees, always come up to them to leeward; it is a pitiful performance, for as soon as they try to get round the sail they are hurled away down wind again. I ran the ship off dead so as to eliminate the eddy wind as far as I could and the little emigrant dropped on deck. I was surprised to see in what good order his feathers were, for he had rested, to my knowledge, twice, floating on the water, on the second occasion for about half a minute; and the sea was pretty rough. He kept his wings half outspread as I think all land birds do when they fall into the sea, and did not have much difficulty about rising again. He came down into the cabin but would not stay there long, and berthed for the night under the spare spars. Unfortunately, when I came to set the foretopsails in the small hours of next morning a downhaul got under one of the spars and gave it a shake which frightened our visitor, and he flew over the side and was no more seen. These creatures are incredibly stupid when they get on shipboard; as soon as they are at all rested they are in a hurry to start off again, though they do not know in which direction the shore lies and have no earthly chance of getting there. I imagine the number of New Zealand species that have been carried to Patagonia is infinitesimal; they will not stand the monotony of the long voyage.

This day I again and for the third time crossed the 180th meridian, got on the right side, that is the western side of the world, and knew that I was going home the shorter way. It was again the 24th of October, as it was yesterday, but I was getting so much accustomed to having two Fridays in a week that I found the Date Line no more trouble than Summer Time. It was also my best day's run this side of the Horn, 173 miles to wit. The wind and sea were moderate enough, and so was L., one of my new helmsmen. M. was better, but it was obvious this was not going to be a very quick passage. I did not even know whether it was going to be a very safe passage, so I took the precaution of lashing on deck a tin of storm-oil (as alleged; it was lucky I never had to use it, for it had absolutely no effect on the waves. Moreover, some leaked out, and fetched all the pitch out of the deck seams. It was the only unsatisfactory thing that I got from the otherwise excellent ship-chandler's at Auckland), and of seeing that the sea anchor could be made available without infinite time and trouble. These things were much more easily done since I had abolished the boat and cut down the deck cargo to the barest necessities; by the time I was a fortnight out I had cleared the main deck so thoroughly that it was a promenade and not an obstacle race. For the comfort and safety of the promenaders I had the sweeps lashed between the main and mizzen rigging; by neglect they were put wrong end first and the mainsheet block hit the blade of one and broke it right off. After that we did not have any topgallant rail till we had finished with the Southern Ocean.

I was now on or near the 38th parallel, the latitude in which I had made my best runs in the Indian Ocean. But here in the Pacific I find in my log repeated entries, up to the 4th of November, when I got into the Roaring Forties, such as, "After two days of light north-westerly airs a breeze from the southward. In topsails and flying-jib for the heavier puffs." This was very different from what I had written nine months before: "Steady northerly breeze and moderate sea, ship doing 8 knots under four lowers and flying-jib" (the latter sail had not then been given substantive rank), followed next day by, "Strong south-west gale, running at $7\frac{1}{2}$ knots under jib and foresail." All the indications were for a light-weather passage, but, if the sea was as moderate as the wind, an average quick passage.

Naturally at this time of year, the early summer, when

the ice would probably be at its farthest northern limit, there was no question of steering a Great Circle course, or anything like it; but a Mercator course towards the Horn was well clear of the danger area. I did not, however, steer exactly along this, for as there was a possibility of getting through the Straits of Magellan I felt that I could afford to lay her off for the broadside of Tierra del Fuego, somewhere between the two, and in fact I was never more than 50 miles either side of this course, which eventuated almost by chance, for there was no conscious striving after it. Long ago, when I was running down the Trades in the North Atlantic, I said a small boat did not make courses like this; it can be imagined how much less sea there was in the Roaring Forties of the Pacific when a course like this was actually made. I have tried to extract from my log any evidence that this was due to skilful dealings with the wandering cyclone, but in vain; it appears that I said, "These are westerly winds and I will steer S. 76° E.," and did so. I also said, when I took my departure from New Zealand, "I will get to Cape Horn in forty days," which, seeing that the distance by the course I had set was over 5,000 miles, demanded a slightly higher average speed than I had yet made between any two ports; but I did it with comparative ease. In fact I simply threw away three days, one by bad temper and two by laziness.

The first was a real tragedy. On the afternoon of the 16th of November in lat. 47½° S., a moderate northerly breeze and an almost imperceptible sea, I was doing well over 8 knots with every stitch of canvas set. The weather looked so settled that I felt almost certain of a record day's run and very hopeful of reaching the 200 miles. It was magnificent sailing, though from aft we hardly realized the vessel was doing anything out of the ordinary, so clean does she leave the water behind her. But look forward and you would realize the force of her going. As the wind was nearly on the beam she was not so much down by the head as usual, and was only pushing the top part of the ocean from her bows, but so fierce was her thrust that the lee bow-wave boiled up to the knight-heads, and a far-spreading rainbow played on the fine dust of water into which it was shattered. Alas! just before midnight I was awakened by a thunderous slatting of canvas, and rushed on deck to find the ship run up in the wind and the foresail and topsails all aback. The steering chains had parted, and I had to take in all the square canvas and the gaff-topsail and heave-to for investigation and repairs. My first showed my second to be a troublesome little job. The thread on the tightening screw had stripped, and in order to replace it with a few spare links or shackles, which would have done just as well, I had to take out the broken part. When I saw that this would have to be done with a hacksaw I knew it was no use thinking about record runs and went to bed again, hoping that I would be in a better frame of mind after breakfast next morning, for a bad temper comes expensive in saw blades.

I might of course have done a temporary repair in a few minutes, but in those usually stormy waters I did not want to risk even for half a day anything unsound; I might have been risking the ship for the sake of a few extra miles; and in any case when I had to do the job properly the conditions would probably not have been so favourable.

It was not very easy to get that broken screw adrift;

I had to curl myself, or as much of myself as would go, into the cockpit, and reach for my work two feet away under the beams of the poop-deck, which were about eleven inches above the floor; and much of that was blocked by wedges I had put in to hold the tiller steady. Then to make a new pin I had to file down, thread and make a nut for a bolt of an unusual size. So now you know why I did not start till after breakfast nor finish before noon; and why we only ran 130 miles that day instead of 200. You may also remark that I was more than three weeks out and more than half-way to the Horn, so that if this accident were a valid excuse for a night of rest the occasion was very suitable for it. The wind was gradually increasing (next day we ran 160 miles, the mainsail being stowed for half of it), and we might be in for a spell of hardship for which we should gladly be fresh.

As a matter of fact before the end of the week I had another accident. The sea was rather steep, so I was steering right before it, and the wind was rather fresh and right aft, so I took in the mainsail and mizzen. Straightway the foresail began to gape at all its seams, and I had it down and unbent it in a hurry before it went to pieces. This left only the jib set, which I sheeted flat a little to port, and this with the wheel lashed with a spoke of port helm kept the sail from shaking, while we got the foresail down into the cabin. There was a big job before us; it was a machine-stitched sail, and the twine in these stands out more prominently than that in handwork, besides being lighter and generally, I think, of inferior strength. Not only the sailmaker, but also the cobbler and the tailor will tell you that the most important quality of machine-thread is that it should render smoothly through the machine; for which purpose they so treat the good rough stuff chemically and mechanically as to take all the strength out of it. In addition to that, in a machine-stitched sail the seams are more liable to chafe, and *Saoirse's* foresail is particularly susceptible in this respect, for her forestay is very vertical and therefore the sail bears heavily on it. We had to side-seam all the bunt, and in a good many other places repairs were necessary; even, for instance, where the soft brails had lain across it.

For the next fortnight a good foresail would be a far more important asset than anything else; I therefore turned all hands on to mending it, to the exclusion of sailing the ship, which was allowed to drift along under bare poles. Even at night, when we could not see properly to mend the sail, I regret to say that we did not set the mainsail, but all turned in. No one was particularly keen about watchkeeping; there was a nasty steep sea which was throwing sprays about, half a gale of wind, and odd showers of hail. We spun out that job over most of two days, making only 90-mile runs.

On the 24th of November I crossed the 50th parallel of latitude, the last stage of the progressive frightfulness with which the Southern Ocean threatens the voyager; the Ocean which I have talked about before, but had not really entered till to-day, defined by the hydrographer as all those seas lying to the southward of the three stormy Capes. It is certainly the classical idea of Oceanus, the great river running (and it does run at quite a fair speed) round the limits of the world; the ideal highway one might think for all ships bound from West to East. But it is really a fraud. It is very inadequately defined, but that does not matter. If it is not a literary rather than a geographical expression, it is subjective rather than objective. It is not, as I once used to think, all the part South of the dotted line which wanders round the lower part of a terrestrial globe; that only marks off the area in which you meet ice. It is, if it has a geographical existence, all that, and also the little areas round the Cape, the Snares and the Horn, where, not being allowed to plague ships with icebergs, it intensifies its other plagues. But to most people it is just the name they call anything they dislike very much. We stood by generally to reef the mainsail and otherwise disarm the tempest; but for the rest of the week this was no worse than any other part of the seas, and my principal business was about the topsails. I could not believe that the wind was going to be lighter and steadier here than in the earlier part of the passage, and quite unnecessarily hauled those topsails down every time a cloud passed over us. I did not get very much help from the crew. L., who had been round here often enough before, but was the worst afflicted with latitude disease —it could not have been anything else, for there was no wind or sea to speak of on that day—growled something about "In my last ship we should be under lower topsails." I made the obvious retort, "So should we, for we do not make 150-day passages like the C—— (his last ship). Jump forward and set them." With it all we made mighty poor runs, for though I set those topsails pretty frequently I was not really much better than my crew and took them in just as often. Besides, we had accumulated a portentous crop of weeds. All her loafing in tropical waters had not fouled the ship as much as five weeks' smart sailing down South; it may be that this part of the sea is full of particularly adhesive spores, but I think the fault really lay with some supposedly anti-fouling composition I got as a cheap bargain in Auckland. This matter of paint is really a great nuisance. It is sold in one-hundredweight drums, enough to last me a year, so when I have taken a few pounds out, there goes back to my forepeak, for I have no other place roomy enough to stow it, that confounded drum not properly closed, with the paint, if happily it stays inside, gradually congealing; and if unhappily it capsizes, oozing all over my sails; or alternatively I give away three-quarters of the contents to someone who can much better afford to buy it than I can. So wherever possible I try to get a lick of paint from someone who already has a drum open; but not at Auckland now.

In view of the possibility of meeting ice in these high latitudes I instituted an eight-hourly routine of taking air and sea temperatures. If one believed the Fahrenheit thermometer (which I did not, for I thought the cold was extremely severe) one might be encouraged by the comparatively mild figures of 48° or thereabouts to suppose that the rigours of this passage had been exaggerated, but I am afraid that the crew, who wanted encouragement just as much as I did, were just as sceptical about the thermometer. L. and M., natives of the inclement Province of Munster, and old seamen, had often been in worse climates, but everybody had told me that K., the Tongan, would die long before he reached the Horn. Certainly he did not look as if he liked snowstorms, but he did not complain about them as the others did—as if I could arrange weather to their liking —and he was always the first man on deck at a call for all hands and generally got the wettest and nastiest job.

CAPE HORN

If by reason of our latitude we were getting rather discouraged, there was an encouraging feature about our longitude. On the day we crossed the 50th parallel I set the clocks six hours slow of Greenwich time, and it was a symbol that I was half-way home. Not of course in point of time or of distance, but very certainly in point of effort; in a week I ought to be in the Atlantic, and once there I was to all intents and purposes at home; well, anyway it was a smooth-water trip all the way home. Meanwhile I was more than 800 miles from Cape Horn and more than 500 from Cape Pillar, at the entrance of the Magellan Straits; and those were not at all smooth-water trips. Nor were the omens favourable. There was an enormous school of black-fish around us, and whalers say that whales mean ice; at any rate the best years for whaling are those in which the ice spreads far North. My apprehensions, however, were vain; when I said an enormous school of black-fish I did not know what whales in bulk looked like. I would amend the epithet to "moderate," after seeing the small whales called minkes in the Schollaert Channel, and that in a year when the district was very free from ice. The other omen was a really enormous quantity of Prions and Cape pigeon. I say that even after seeing Cape pigeon attending the obsequies of fifteen whales in Port Foster. This is supposed to indicate bad weather in the neighbourhood; but I think now it indicates rather that what is food for the black-fish is food for the Cape pigeon. I imagine that these omens are interpreted as the Sailing Directions are written, by a Trade Union of South Seamen in order to warn off the course those who have not been duly apprenticed to it; or perhaps that sailors' yarns are required by the landlords of their inns and the publishers of their adventures to be highly spiced for the good of trade. Contrariwise I say that no adventures are to be found in the Southern Ocean, for it is the most startling thing I can think of to say about it. I question whether the poor traveller can justly be blamed for untruthfulness, when lies are expected of him.

If the birds were not an omen, at least they were an entertainment. We had not seen land or land animals for a month, and this incursion of life, even of pelagic life, was welcome. Most conspicuous of course on account of his great size was the Wandering Albatross. That is what I call him when he is sweeping in wide circles around the ship without moving a muscle. But when he is afloat, or comes very near one, the sailors' name of "Cape Sheep" seems more appropriate, for he is a woolly beast and clothed with very untidy ragged wool at that, while his face is, except for a beak more than a foot long, distinctly ovine. All this woolliness makes him very light for his bulk, and in consequence he drifts about in a ridiculous manner on the water and occasionally capsizes in a rough sea. He seemed to me to be singularly careless about the set of his feathers: one would suppose that a bird which spent most of his life in the air would be very particular about his wings, and I was much surprised to see him boxing his wife's ears with them. But he does not beat the water with them when he rises from it, which he does in this wise. He turns head to wind, spreads his wings, slowly lifts his right foot and places it on the surface, then does the same with his left, and lastly draws both up under him, and there he is. No need to flap or kick as lesser fowls do, his system of levitation supersedes the cruder methods. And in some marvellous manner, for the secret of which I am sure any aeroplane builder would give his fortune, he goes on rising or travelling in any direction without moving his wings for an apparently endless period. For a long time I believed that the Mother Carey's Chicken, at the other end of the scale of size, had the power of levitation even more developed, and never used the sea at all except to walk upon; whence his name of Stormy Petrel, or Little Peter. But I saw these butterflies of the sea sharing the refuse of a whale factory with the Cape pigeon, and then they could not even walk on the water, much less fly. Still in normal conditions I never saw one swimming, out of all the thousands that accompanied us. It must be a very wearing life, for they never rise more than a few inches above the surface, and as the waves may be rising twenty feet and moving with corresponding speed in any direction, great vigilance and agility is required to avoid getting knocked over by the breaking crests, though of course the birds can walk up the unbroken slopes. But all the oceanic birds are wonderfully skilful at dodging seas, even the albatross sometimes comes down to amaze one by his swoops along the narrow rolling valleys. The low flying habit seems to be proportionate to the smallness of the birds; next to the Mother Carey's Chicken comes the Prion, who keeps about the height of an average flying-fish, which he would resemble greatly but for his erratic zigzag flight. I think they feed on things so small that even their keen sight could not pick them out from a considerable elevation; and it is even said that the reason the Stormy Petrel likes a good breeze is that he picks animalculæ out of the spindrift.

Hitherto I had kept an open mind as to which side

of Tierra del Fuego I should go, but with Cape Pillar only 200 miles away I had to decide on a course. I knew pretty accurately where I was then, but my dead-reckoning is not such that I could be sure where I should be in two days if I got no more observations, for in that latitude and in two days I might easily be run badly out of my course by heavy weather. I wanted to steer a good course, for there was only one mark on the coast of which I could be sure, the Evangelistas Lighthouse, in the middle of the entrance to the Magellan Straits, since the mountains are, according to the Sailing Directions, generally hidden in clouds, and therefore the pretty pictures of Landfall Island, Cape Pillar, or Isla Contreras would be of no practical value; and on the not improbable chance of a south-westerly gale, which would bring clear weather, it would be equally useless to me to identify them if the sea were so bad that I could not weather the dangers that front Dislocation Harbour, the Straits, and Golfo Sarmiento. Nor if I were steering for the lighthouse could I afford to overrun my distance without seeing it, for there were 20 miles of reefs between it and Westminster Hall, when the safe fairway begins. Once in that it is, I am told, physically impossible to get into trouble with the land, the only danger being the appalling squalls that fall upon one down the mountain gullies. They might dismast one, but they would not drive one ashore, for in the narrower reaches, so my informant said, they would be blowing straight through the channel; and in any case one would bounce off the kelp without doing any damage. This much I disbelieve, for my impression of kelp is that one would stick in it long before one collected a solid enough cushion to do any bouncing off.

But Lord! With what timidity does one navigate after two generations of dependence on tug-boats. Once upon a time big unhandy square-riggers used to go through these Straits both ways. Now indeed the Sailing Directions say that a vessel may pass through from West to East, though nothing but smooth water would be gained. The Sailing Directions are grossly utilitarian. Oh, you yachtsmen who make an annual pilgrimage to the West of Scotland, and rarer ones to the Fjords of Norway, would you not sacrifice a day or two, not for the sake of smooth water and the best china and glass on the dinner table, but to see great mountains plunging down into the sea between huge mountains clothed with evergreen Antarctic beech? Not if you have read the literature on the district. Sir Martin Conway, who came specially to climb Monte Sarmiento, never saw its summit clear of clouds; this same Sailing Directions, the *South American Pilot*, Part II (which is my authority for all the more improbable statements that I shall make in this chapter), thus describes the appearance of the land behind Cape Pillar: "a very high and almost level tableland, the rugged peaks of which are hidden by the heavy clouds which hang over them." When I go sightseeing it is for the sake of the peaks, and I do not consider a level tableland much of a place to go looking for scenery in; and as the weather was settling into thick misty rain it was not much of a day to go looking for the Straits of Magellan all along a lee shore. So I kept away to the south-eastward, at a distance of a couple of hundred miles off the coast; a nice comfortable berth offshore; room enough to lie-to through a three days' south-westerly gale.

Some critic may remind me that I have claimed for

Saoirse that she will maintain her position in a gale. Why then this demand for a couple of hundred miles of sea-room? The home yachtsman, who navigates a familiar coast, well-lit and well provided with harbours, is sometimes apt to scoff at the deep-water man's fear of a lee shore. But only those who have experienced a really bad sea know how helpless a small craft is in it, even if her sails and gear are intact; and, if she were driven ashore on any of the 350 miles between Cape Pillar and the Horn, the chances of her crew landing alive, and being rescued by the Chilean patrol before they starved, would be very small. There was no need for me to run things fine, and so I did not. I got to the southward pretty quickly and just as quickly the cold increased, though this was summer, the last day of November, and I was no farther from the Equator than is Rathlin Island; and the prospect became more and more depressing.

The sea, so long deep blue sparkling with silver, had changed to a dull and ugly black, the sky was drawing up a veil of indefinite cloud, and the brave west wind that had served me for forty days was momentarily dropping. The water dried on decks and sails and ropes, and drying left a grey crust; the light faded out of the heavens and left a greyness than which anything else seemed more luminous; the very foam on the wave-crests was no longer white but grey; the greyness pressed upon me so that it hurt. I left the wheel to K. and went below to get a bright orange scarf; it was no good, on deck it was as colourless as anything else. K.'s face too was by now grey, and small wonder, for this was the coldest day of the passage. The ship and all in her appeared by the unnatural light as pale ghosts against the murk. The barometer was tumbling down, and in a word it meant snow.

In this calm the waves, lacking the guidance of the breeze, fell out of their ordered ranks and ran anywhither in confused heaps; we were dizzied by the violence with which the ship was carried by their swing backwards and forwards, from side to side, with slamming of sails and creaking of gear. But before long the ridges of the swell showed darker against the sky to the eastward, small pyramids of water rose and toppled down their steep sides, and the wide sweep of the spars through the air made the rigging shriek with a note alternately high and low; a breeze had come. It came straight from the glaciers of the Fuegian mountains, and with it came little flakes of snow, wet snow that trickled down the canvas, as grey as the sails and spars on which it built up a half-transparent film. However, with any sort of wind, unpleasant as a snowy head wind was, I had command of the ship again. I reefed the mainsail, stowed the jib, a nasty wet job, and the temperature of the water was 44° and of the air 42°, and hove-to. The wind freshened, but the fresher it blew the easier the ship rode, and the better the galley stove-pipe drew. I do not know how hard it blew, nor for how long, for we all slept well that night.

How pleasant it is to lie in bed till seven instead of turning out at four! How much better is one's morning tea when brought to one's cabin than when snatched precariously in the chart-room! And how extremely tactful was K., who, when he brought it, merely informed me that we had now a fair wind, and said nothing about how long we had been sailing in the direction of Valparaiso. But so slowly that it made no matter; and if one is going to take a night of rest one may as well take the whole night. I dislike doing things before breakfast, but I regret that if I indulge in my tastes it sometimes means a record in my log-book of only 11 miles.

Through a day of moderate but gloomy weather the wind and the barometer were constantly changing and foretold more dirt, which came in the small hours of next morning with a southerly squall. There was really not much force in it, and very little sea; I was south of the 56th parallel and could make a fair wind of it, but the wretched L., who had long been developing a tendency to let the ship broach to, was now making a habit of it. I did not see the fun of taking his wheel, so I took in the foresail and made the ship fool-proof for him. I confess it gave me some satisfaction to see him setting the sail again in his watch below, for I was getting rather tired of doing all the work.

We were now an unnecessary distance off the land; I had intended to pick up the Islas Ildefonso, and that would have been an extravagantly safe landfall, for I might quite well have gone close enough in to see York Minster and the wonderful scenery of the coast, but the current, or perhaps that tiresome instinct which always puts me out of my reckoning when I approach land, set me some 20 miles farther South, so that I passed my mark in the haze and the first thing I saw was Diego Ramirez.

At the same time I began seeing gleams of white among the clouds that hung on the northern horizon, and as these retreated a flash of light shot out of the grey bank, the rays of the sun reflected from some great ice-slope far distant. Very soon white shapes detached themselves from the purple background, probably the

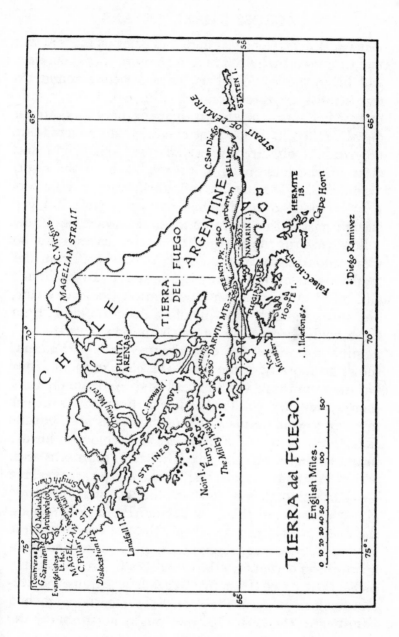

TIERRA del FUEGO.

English Miles.

0 10 20 30 40 50   100   150

Darwin Range, 7,000 feet high and 80 or 90 miles away; but who could tell? for here a mountain of 3,000 feet will breed glaciers. And as the sun swung round towards the West those great ice-cliffs which had, while he was behind them, shown their southern faces to me only by reflected light off the clouds, so steep were they, now caught his direct rays and stood out bright and clear on the huge mass of French Peak on the right, gradually fading away into infinite distance and the perpetual vapours of the Pacific Coast on the left. But as I steered past Diego Ramirez to the eastward, and now a little towards the north also, for the first time for so many months, the lower clouds rolled back from the foothills and from over my head, and I saw the black cliffs of Hoste Island standing firm on the level water, and they, and even the ridiculous little islands of Ildefonso, which were dipping on the horizon, became the dominant feature of the landscape, with the eternal snows no more than the icing of a cake to them. Your big mountains are very jealous, and immediately hide themselves when you look at lower things. So I turned my eyes towards a place where there was no competition, the nearest rocks, snow-free and coloured by the bright sunlight, on our port bow; the group of islands which terminates America; a warm, pleasant place lapped by smooth seas under a blue sky, or so it seemed after the snows of the grey Pacific. Perhaps here I do the Pacific less than justice; only the last two days were grey, and only a few hours were snowy; we had been favoured as perhaps no ship ever was before by the elements. But by contrast this weather was quite marvellous for lat. 56° S. in the Atlantic. Or perhaps, having admitted a Southern Ocean, I ought not to allow the

Atlantic to extend beyond Staten Island; but I knew at least that when I had altered course that little to the northward I had crossed the three undeniable oceans of the world.

Very soon the jagged outlines of Hermite Island near at hand threw the paler hills of Hoste back to their proper distance, and the great mountains now standing dark against the sunset came forward over them and regained all their former magnificence. And before nightfall everything else was dominated by the steep black cone of Cape Horn itself.

This is not a Cape, but an island, and derives its name not from its shape, but from the enterprising Dutchman who discovered it. For a great many years navigators believed that Tierra del Fuego was connected with the Antarctic continent, and the Dutch Government, on this assumption, granted a monopoly of all the trade "beyond the Straits." Captain Van Hoorn, having a lawyer's mind, went round outside and broke into the monopoly of the West Coast, supposing rightly that in those days of poor communications no one was likely to examine him except in the Narrows. A hundred years later he was forgotten, for on a chart of that period the name is placed on False Cape Horn, which is very much more horned than the real one, and spelled with a single o. Such is fame. But when you see it you have no doubt which is the greatest cape of the world. Its peak is no more than 1,400 feet high, but it has no rivals near, and all that height plunges down almost sheer to the South. One could hardly design a more suitable finish to a great continent.

Some captious reader will remark that I saw a rather improbable quantity of the Chilean coast in one afternoon, and might even suspect me of copying more than the heights and names of mountains out of that *South America Pilot* that lies before me; and I confess that when I look at the chart I am surprised at the wealth of detail in my recollections. It must be remembered, however, that the visibility was exceptionally good, that it was quite light at ten o'clock and never dark all night, and that I was being set to the eastward at the rate of at least 1 knot (I was again more than 20 miles out of my reckoning, and in spite of light winds and a foul bottom I logged 140 miles next day).

The wind fell lighter and lighter and veered more northerly, we did little more than drift with the current, and it was obviously impossible to get through the Strait of Le Maire, which, besides being the shortest way to Montevideo, led up along a weather shore, so that beyond it I should be assured of smooth water.

This morning I had confirmation of my observations on the visibility of objects at sea; the most conspicuous thing was Bell Mountain in Tierra del Fuego, about 60 miles away, and only 2,600 feet high. I could have seen Monte Sarmiento yesterday but for the clouds on it.

And by next morning we had drifted as far as Staten Island and enjoyed the panorama of that amazing coast at a distance of 10 to 15 miles. It is the most fantastic wall of rock ever created, being some 40 miles long and so thin in places that there are windows through it, in others so substantial that peaks rise from it 3,000 feet above the sea. In general outline it looks like the coarsest kind of cross-cut saw. But when one gets near enough one sees that the mountains are not everywhere strictly vertical, but in places are covered with luxuriant vegetation, green all the year round, where in the tops of the tallest trees innumerable cormorants build their nests and over the flowering undergrowth swarms of humming-birds hover. On the rocky parts of course are penguins and albatrosses, as found in any island in 55° S. The fact is not officially admitted, but it is notorious that a warm current washes the shores of the West Falkland Island, and it probably extends as far as Staten Island; but I was very much intrigued by the descriptions of birds and flowers so far South and should have liked much to see if they were true; but alas! I had no boat, and I understood that the one inhabitant had emigrated.

By the time I had got clear of Staten Island I thought that it would be a hopelessly long job to try to get to Montevideo, especially as the potatoes and flour were running low. But we could lie our course for the Falkland Islands close-hauled, so considering that after all Montevideo was very much like any other large city, and the Falklands very much unlike any other small country, I made an amusement of a necessity and carried on to the north-eastward.

There was more than weeds keeping the ship back, and next morning I took action in respect of an avoidable cause of delay. Coming on deck I found M., whose wheel it was, steering points off his course with the sails as flat as boards. During the night the wind had come right aft, but he had never troubled to check a foot of sheet, much less to gybe on to the proper course or set any square canvas. This sort of thing had happened so often before, though never so inexcusably, that I declared I would keep no more watches myself if I had to trim sail for everybody else; nor did I, up to Stanley; that was for thirty-six hours.

I wondered that afternoon at the pale green colour

of the sea, for it was not possible that we were so far out of our course as to be over the shoaler part of the Burdwood bank. But I do not believe that even the deepest sea is necessarily dark blue; 200 miles off the Fuegian coast it was black, here it was green, a couple of hundred miles beyond the Falklands it was a pale turquoise, and further on yet a reddish brown—this last caused, I am nearly sure, by whale-feed. As a matter of fact we had been set to the westward, and at midnight made Beauchene Island, the southern outlier of the Islands, close to, rather unexpectedly, but very fortunately, for the coast of the mainland some 40 miles farther North is flat, featureless, and fronted by reefs, and no place for a stranger to make a landfall. So as long as it kept moderately clear (I never saw the Falkland Islands looking anything like Tierra del Fuego, and this morning the hills were almost hidden in clouds) I had no need to identify the low and inconspicuous islands off Lafonia nor to close the shore until I could be sure of where Stanley lay behind the higher land. We carried on to the eastward with a good offing, accompanied by seals rolling over the sea like large porpoises, and penguins like small ones, till I saw a thing I had not seen since leaving New Zealand, a sail coming up astern. There was a smart breeze of wind blowing, as is almost invariably the case here during the daytime. For a space we kept our distance, though the stranger was a schooner four times our size and using an engine; but as the sea rose she overtook us. It was a long time since I had any criterion of the speed we made through the water; now if our bow-wave was anything like that of the *Gwendolin* ranging alongside for a hail (and I suspect it was bigger) we must have looked a pretty sight. She was going to Stanley, so I asked the Captain to arrange for the pilot and the doctor on my behalf, and she went on ahead of us, but not very far ahead as long as we had the wind well aft, for I soon got the top-sails set. But when it came to beating up Port William, the outer harbour, although I had sent down the fore-yard and unrove all the gear I could spare, the weeds crippled the ship so badly that I was much relieved to see the pilot coming out in a good steam-launch (though that launch was rather notorious in the matter of salvage claims) and getting a good tow-rope on board. I need hardly add I was charged nothing for the tow, for this was a different sort of colony that I had come to.

So forty-six days after leaving Auckland I laid the ship on moorings off the dockyard in charge of the Government, and made inquiries about a suitable beach and a suitable tide to clean her bottom. And since I was overwhelmed with offers of hospitality, and since this was the 6th of December and I had spent last Christmas at sea and did not intend to go on to Montevideo, I supposed that the suitable tide would not occur for at least three weeks.

CHAPTER IX

THE FALKLAND ISLANDS

I SUPPOSE the Governor saw me looking with a critical eye on the amenities of Stanley—of which there are none—for he commanded the Seal Protection Cruiser to take me round the coast and demonstrate that not all his domain was desert, a very apt description of the part which is generally seen by visitors. For there is very little visible from the mail-boat anchorage in Fort William except stones and wind; they have, in fact, a particularly vicious kind of wind which is called mail-boat weather. There is no soil, no warmth in the sun, no trees will grow, and only the hardiest weeds; though it is true that a few enthusiasts have constructed gardens in the lee of a stout fence and are even reported to have raised potatoes therein. Most crops are raised under glass; and there are two schools of gardeners. One asserts that sea-gulls drop marrow-bones on one's greenhouse because they think the bone will crack first, and use wire-netting; the other that the birds cannot see the glass and are aiming for the tiled passages, and use green cocoanut matting. But these are trifles; the people live pecuniarily on wool and gastronomically on mutton.

But I was not being sent to study horticulture (which even in the more genial West Falkland is a farce) or to make the acquaintance of the western farmer (who is like any other, only more hospitable), but to see something that I could not see elsewhere; to wit, fur seals and penguins. And because of the fierce and persistent wind round that rocky coast I was very glad to go in someone else's ship, and to lie in my bunk and listen to the wind howling aloft, knowing that someone else was keeping an anchor watch and standing by in the engine-room. One must have been a ship's captain to appreciate being a passenger.

This was a thoroughly yachting trip; we did not steam at night, but anchored opposite some settlement and all went ashore; it is the custom even with passengers in the trading vessels. In a country with only 2,000 inhabitants all told everybody knows everybody else. At this time of year some part of every day is fine, and there is no heavy rain, though often showers; the wind dies down at night; and it is never very cold, though never at all warm. It would be fine winter weather with us, but here it was mid-summer, the week before Christmas. The only difference between summer and winter is in the length of the days.

The scenery of the East Falkland is not impressive, for the hills, though of bold outline, as is always the case with quartzite, are small and scattered, and the whole looks a desolation; but as we opened up the Falkland Sound the mountains were quite fine, though nothing rises much over 2,000 feet. I was forcibly struck by the colouring of it all; it was as wintry-looking a landscape as ever I saw. Hardly a touch of green anywhere, except where a patch of tussac grass survived, and that was but a cold greyish green, for the plant is like the pampas grass, but soft and very sweet for cattle; or where a spring on the hill-side kept a little space round it alive; the rest was blackish fern and diddle-dee (the substitute for heather, but I believe no

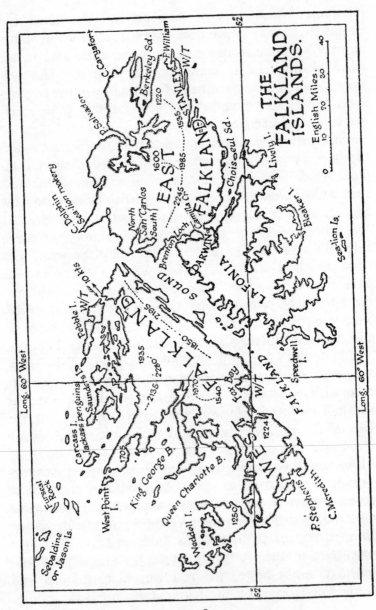

THE
FALKLAND
ISLANDS.

English Miles.
0 10 20 30 40

relative) and the whitish leaves of dead grass. Except of course for the still whiter stones, so white that when the sun fell on them as they streamed in a broad river down from the castellated crags that topped each pyramid peak, one thought that one was looking on the remains of winter snow.

I was coming to a place which was not at all one to explore in a sailing boat—what cowards we are! Till a few years ago it was worked with nothing else—a place with ten-knot tides running through the narrowest and crookedest channels, in which even steamers get aground at times. It is easy enough to see the way at slack water, for all the rocks are liberally buoyed with kelp, but slack water lasts only a minute or two, and when the streams start the kelp is run under and you have no guide except inconspicuous and often distant shore bearings. We went through five of these narrows; one, in which you have to zigzag through a couple of miles of reefs all lying directly across the general course, is of such bad repute that accidents happening there are not covered by any insurance. We took it at slack water; at any other time it is a most exciting performance, as one has to steam full speed to keep command of the ship in the rips and eddies, and only a short and handy vessel can negotiate the turns.

The farther West we got the more grass was apparent, and our anchorage for the night in the beautiful harbour of West Point Island might have been in West Cork. Not only is there more soil here and less wind, but the temperature is much higher; that of the sea water at the time was 52° F. as against 45° in Stanley Harbour. Bonito, a sub-tropical fish, have been caught off the coast; fuchsias grow here, and at some period there were considerable trees, for their partly silicified trunks are buried in a recent deposit on the beach. But what I came to West Point to see was a penguin rookery.

I walked, it seemed, a prodigious way up the hill on this side, and a very short way down on the other; I do not know how many feet I was above the sea when I came to the edge of the cliff and found the penguins there, of all places; not only grown birds, but eggs, and chickens, who would require twice as much food as their parents before they were fledged. There seemed to me to be here two hard questions: first, why do Rock-hopper Penguins make their rookery on the top of a cliff, and second, how do they get up there with the enormous weight of food necessary for their children? On the first question authorities are divided, some maintaining that the rookery was originally on a flat rock near the sea, and that later upheavals, landslips, and other modifications of the form of the earth have left it on a steep rock far away from the sea, the penguins, most conservative of birds, declining to shift for such trivial geological processes. The other school says that they climb up the steepest place they can manage so that the seals shall not follow and eat them. They have, of course, facilitated the way; a penguin road cut up a couple of hundred feet of quartzite cliff is a marvellous piece of engineering.

On the second question the authorities are not helpful, they merely record that the birds do breed and feed their chickens there, as anyone can see; supposing that fish descend like manna for their benefit, which phenomenon neither I nor anyone else have seen. But I think I can guess how it happens. Adjoining the penguin rookery there is always a rookery of mollymawks;

now if there is one bird more than any other unlike the
noisy, quarrelsome little penguin it is that dignified old
gentleman with a spread of wing of 7 feet and a beak
like a pickaxe; and he looks down his long nose at them
accordingly. But he is no good as a fisherman. I suggest
that the penguin catches all the fish for both rookeries,
and the Molly carries it up to both. That explains how
the young penguins are fed. The joint housekeeping
which I have observed further South, where the Blue-
Eyed Cormorant and Ringed Penguin share a rookery,
has, of course, a different origin; there eligible sites free
from snow are so rare that everybody uses them indiscriminately. The Molly performs one other service for
the Rocky Penguins. You may always see him standing
sentry on a stone in the middle of the rookery; he is paid
to keep skua-gulls from stealing chickens. Whatever you
may think about him as a transport agent, there is
nothing more incredible in his capacity of policeman
than in the relations of shark and pilot-fish, or the un-
holy conspiracy of Xiphias and Orca to kill whales;
or, if it comes to that, is anything more incredible than
a penguin?

You will always see the Molly standing on a stone in
the penguin rookery, or on that clay pedestal he calls
his nest in his own, because, like many another large
sea-bird, he cannot rise from the level ground. You
would feel sorry for him when a couple of squabbling
penguins get between his legs and capsize him, to see
him floundering about and stumbling over rocks and
birds, and, one would suppose, grievously injuring his
wings in his efforts to get on his feet again. The signs are
on them; I have seen some birds in a disgracefully
ragged condition; but I suppose they have an enormous

reserve of lifting power. Penguins, on the other hand, have every right to use their flippers, not only to walk with but to fight with, and very effective weapons they are too. They hold you with their beaks, and turning their flippers horizontally belabour you with the cutting forward edge. They have very little manners and no morals; they will fight for another bird's wife, or his egg, or the sticks with which he is building his nest; or if his back is turned will steal any one of the three. They are very affectionate parents, and spoil their children, who have communistic ideas on the subject of property in food. You must not think when you see a half-fledged bird charging through the rookery and pecking at all the elder generation that he is merely out for mischief; he is just hungry (and well he may be, for he is growing visibly) and expects to be fed by a total stranger as soon as by his own parents.

However badly they behave in the family circle, most of them treat larger animals like men and mollymawks respectfully enough. It would be well if mollymawks could read that last sentence, though I do not go so far as the fellow that shot that supercilious bird to teach him the difference between men and penguins. Most penguins are not only respectful but friendly to man, especially if man will scratch the back of their necks, for their legs are too short to do it for themselves. But there is one surly solitary bird who lives in a burrow and brays like a jackass. He bites. I saw him next day, when I went to Carcass Island. I was wandering along the beach, and I treasure two tests of Echinocardium and Austrocidaris as a reminder of how jolly it was to be at the seaside after being so long at sea, when I saw a flock of penguins who ran from me, an action explained

by the fact that they had made themselves so deservedly
unpopular that they did not like to be caught by strangers between their holes and the sea, in which they were
a match for any swimming thing. It is written that these
Jackass Penguins arrange red and white pebbles at the
mouths of their burrows, so that a person walking down-
hill through the rookery shall take warning and not
break through; but I saw no signals, and the first indication of danger was a noise like a reed foghorn on a
lighthouse going off under my feet; so being barefooted
I went round another way, to approach them face to
face.

On this same island I saw yet another kind of penguin, the Gentoo, whose rookeries are established on
the slopes, or even the summits of grassy hills. A walk
of two or three miles, an ascent of as many hundred feet,
is nothing to them. Their road is not cut in the hard
rock, but laid with short smooth turf, and on it two files
are continually marching, one up, one down; the birds
at regular intervals, with their heads in the air and their
flippers slightly thrown back for the sake of balance; a
fine show indeed, but you must not hustle them or drive
them into the rough, for their legs are very short
and their feet very big and they cannot see where
they are going and trip up over roots and stones and
scuttle away on all fours in a most undignified manner.
But your penguin is very nearly a quadruped; I have
seen some (I think they were Adelie Penguins) crossing
a snow-covered ice-floe, and they just lay prone on it
and sculled themselves along with their flippers. There
are no tricks in the way of locomotion unknown to the
Antarctic Penguins, who travel fabulous distances over
the ice; I saw an extemporized road from a rookery of

Ringed Penguins on Anvers Island; it was a toboggan run down a snow-slope sufficiently fast to shoot the birds that used it over some very nasty rocks at the bottom of a 50-foot sea-cliff. What happened to the pioneers I do not know, but you cannot hurt a penguin any more than you can a seal.

I have made the Rockhopper Penguins establish their rookeries 200 feet up a cliff to avoid the seals; I have made the Gentoo Penguins climb 500 feet of mountain for that purpose; I have put the Jackass Penguin in burrows (and I wish he may be buried in them), but I have not explained why seals and killer whales do not devour them in the water. They cannot; nothing in the world swims like a penguin. I could not see how they do it, the motion is too rapid; but I fancy it is entirely done with the flippers, their feet (for their tails are only used, like that of the kangaroo, to sit upon) merely acting as rudders. And those that only know *Phoca vitulina* of our coasts will perhaps wonder why they are so desperately afraid of seals, ashore. Far South, where one sees penguin rookeries at the water's edge, the seals are as incompetent rock-climbers as is our common seal at home. I confess to having roused a Weddell seal from his sleep, just to see how he, having no obvious legs or arms, moved down the beach. I had heard that he had moved like a caterpillar, but a caterpillar has legs, ten of them; this one, after rolling over on his back to have a look at me, went down like a slug tied up in a bag. So he could not catch penguins. But the seals in the Falkland Islands are very different. I did not see any elephants, but our business was with fur seals and sea-lions. We were to visit a rock off the Sebaldine Islands, on which there is a rookery (penguins is rooks and seals is rooks), for the first lieutenant of the cruiser to take a census of the fur seals and to massacre the sea-lions; for the chief engineer to take photographs of the proceedings; and for me to be introduced to these animals, about which I had very vague ideas.

We landed on a narrow sloping ledge, overhung by a great slab of rock of which the upper surface was invisible, and sidled along under it in single file. When our leader was high enough to see what was above us, he sang out that there were two lions up there, and that he was going to shoot them. Now the one place to avoid if you are going to startle a sea-lion is directly between him and the water, for he will go over you like a steam-roller, and that is exactly where three of us were stuck behind the chief who was training his camera on the beasts. I did not see how we should be much better off if they were killed, for they would certainly roll down the slope, and a sea-lion weighs half a ton alive or dead. Fortunately the Chief finished his pictures and we could move on a little before the avalanche fell.

The rocks rose before us in a series of tilted sheets of massive quartzite, polished by generations of seals to the slipperiness of ice, and here at any rate nothing could fall unexpectedly on our heads, for we could see all clear before us up to the skyline along which huge black Sphinx-like forms sat with their noses seven feet up in the air. What we had to guard against was falling unexpectedly on top of a seal. The bulk of them were lying in the troughs of the rocks and where the escarpments were undercut at the bottom were often invisible from above. It was disconcerting when we started to climb down one of these to see a great ugly face issuing from the rock and curling up to ask us with a roar what we were doing there. It is well that the cliffs should be strictly vertical and at least 8 feet high; this discourages them from following one with supplementary questions. The prudent man sees to his line of retreat; on level ground he can run as fast as a seal, but on their own rocks he should allow himself a good start, for the seal is rather short in the wind and does not pursue one far. We were fortunate in finding very few clap-matches—the females—at home, for they resented our interference with their nurseries and they can run much faster than their husbands, and bite just as hard. Nor were the pups backward in this respect; they are the most charming babies in the world, to look at, but have a fine equipment of teeth. Their fathers, the wigs, were supposed to be looking after the nurseries, but were neglecting their duties shamefully; with these animals the mating season follows closely on the birth of the pup, and they were fighting for a space on which to collect their harem of twenty or thirty wives, or resting after their fights. Meanwhile the unfortunate pups were getting kicked all over the place; they did not seem to mind falling about on the rocks, for you cannot hurt a seal, but it must be a troublesome job for their mothers to find them again, and a good many must get drowned. Young seals have to be made to swallow stones before they can take the water, otherwise they go down by the head; indeed many authorities say that no seal can swim without ballast; but others that they use the stones to knock off intestinal worms.

There were on this little rock alone some 2,000 fur-seal pups, postulating an equal number of clapmatches, most of whom were away fishing, and over a hundred wigs, but no young males; at which I did not wonder, seeing those scarred old heroes watching for any possible competitor in the marriage market. They are no beauties at the best of times, but now they were a shocking sight and the island was running with their blood.

The sea-lion, being monogamous, does not have to face such fierce competition, and his battles are less bloody. Nature gave him an even uglier face, but his wife is just as handsome and graceful as the fur seal's. I do not suppose that he would attack a man without provocation; the awkward situations arise if one stumbles over him in a cleft of the rocks, or comes face to face with him in the tussac grass; for he will make straight for the sea and is not gentle in removing obstacles from his path.

After Christmas, searching as usual for a reason to delay my start, I decided that I had not made a proper job of scrubbing my hull, and was advised to go for that purpose to San Carlos in the Falkland Sound, where there was more range of tide. The advice was, I think, just as much an excuse as my taking of it; the people of the Middle West did not see why the people of the Far West should get all the credit for hospitality; for their tides were no better than those in Stanley. Besides, they wanted their mail—three of the most portentous sacks which I have ever seen, which had been refused on the score of their size by two other vessels. I dislike coasting voyages and side-shows generally, but it was a case of going to San Carlos or going to sea, so I chose the former, and certainly in the way of scenery was well repaid. On the way there, on a calm morning (the weather was out of its proper order; that afternoon there was a fresh North-Easter), we had a sea-lioness in company, swimming round and diving under the ship, rolling and gambolling in the water, a beautiful sight and the only time I ever saw a seal showing off so exclusively for our benefit.

The land about the Falkland Sound, though not so good as that farther west, grows enough grass to support a few cattle as well as innumerable geese. These geese, after the wind, are the second curse of the country, and a price is put on their heads. All one can say about them is that they are easy to shoot and good to eat. The sea-lions are the third curse; they destroy the tussac grass, which is becoming quite scarce, and, with the help of penguins and cormorants, eat all the fish that approaches the coast. All one can say about them is that they are full of oil; a large drifter can steam 7 miles on one lion. But the Government will not allow them to be boiled, supposing, probably correctly, that too many fur seals, which are so   protected, would be killed by mistake.

A little way up the beautiful San Carlos River, which winds between steep bluffs covered with fern and pale-green cushions of balsam, with here and there a bush of white veronica sheltering in the hollow of the cliffs, we tied up to the jetty and discharged those monstrous mail-bags. An expedition arrived from the neighbouring settlement, San Carlos South, across the mountains, looked at those bags, and invited me to visit that place next; and the manager of San Carlos North piloted me round there. And when I was at San Carlos South the people of Darwin rang me up to say that they were sending me a pilot to bring me their way; and I certainly wanted that pilot, for I never saw such an unlikely looking place as that they expected me to get into. Brenton Loch itself was a horribly narrow place boiling with tide; and a fresh breeze was blowing up it, and it was eight miles long, and therefore the head of it would have been a mighty rough anchorage. But the pilot said he was going to put me into a perfectly sheltered berth where yachts always lay, and by the time I saw what kind of a place this was I was too late to prevent his going in; so we gave a yaw to port and a yaw to starboard and let go both anchors and all the halliards and bumped off the bank to starboard on to the bank to port, and hauled off that by a line across the creek; and there we were moored, rather breathless and not too well pleased to have a number of spectators, in this very perfect anchorage on one side or another of which we were aground at every low water.

The other mile of road (there is one in Stanley, with a Ford on it) is in the neighbourhood of Darwin, but not on this side of it, a fact which did not prevent the other Ford from coming across country to fetch me. The Sailing Directions appeared to be to keep the starboard wheels in the cut-away bog and the port wheels in the watercourse. It was just as quick as walking, if not so comfortable.

All this time I was wondering how I was going to get out of Camilla Creek. I could not hope for another North-Easter; the last of the ebb and a calm, conditions necessary for towing out, never coincided, but my bold Pilot reckoned he could smell a slant of wind on which we could sail out, getting enough way on in the basin to shoot head to wind through the narrows. Blessed is the ketch rig with a strong wind against a strong tide in such a place! I had plenty of help to run the mainsail up as soon as the anchor was away, and under that and staysail the ship ran some fifty yards up the river, stayed round in her own length (a ketch so canvassed will do this) and reached down for the entrance like a railway train while we set the jib and mizzen, and so out on the rushing ebb. It was an even more breathless performance than coming in. I thought that invaluable pilot deserved a trip to Stanley, and took him there.

When I got there I found another good reason for not being in a hurry to sail for home. I was commanded to go on the mail steamer to the South Shetlands and those parts of Antarctica which are used by whalers, and as she was not due to sail for some time my poor yacht got rather more of a refit than she generally enjoyed— but then she did not generally get a Government Dockyard to do it for her. As I was putting on the finishing touch the Colonial Secretary came down to pass the time of day. Now my finishing touch was a little bit of carved and gilt gingerbread work to replace that which had been knocked off her stern in Durban. From time to time I had started it, but as sure as I did so some awful thing would happen as an omen that I should never get home, and the badge of the Royal Irish Yacht Club would add nothing to the boat's selling value in New Zealand. But now I felt so sure that I was home that I finished and fixed it, with no disastrous consequences. The Colonial Secretary, seeing me at this kind of work, bade me design a Coat of Arms for the Colony (for he had fallen foul of the College of Heralds) and I, wishing to repay the Government in some small degree for the work their dockyard artificers had done for me, without regard to what was thought of my trick in Queen Victoria Street, had to comply.

Very soon I was embarked again as a passenger in the converted trawler that carries passengers and mails to the Far South, together with the Colonial Secretary, who was going to deliver official castigation to a certain Scottish whale-factory—(these are licensed by the State on condition that they show a reasonable output of oil for whales killed. If there is evidence of a waste of whales the licence is withdrawn. This is clearly necessary when the annual catch approaches twelve thousand whales. Needless to say, the licence fees pay the whole cost of the Government of the Falkland Islands)—and the Colonial Surgeon, who was going to inspect the local hospital.

As we left cold and stormy Stanley astern, travelling 200 miles a day to the southward, the wind dropped, the sea became like a lake, and the sun shone for the whole day of eighteen hours or more. I was told that this is expected in the summer, south of the 60th parallel, with the exception that over the South Shetlands there are usually and over one particular island there are always clouds and foul weather. So on the morning that we made the land at O'Brien Island all I saw was a lofty black cliff seamed with snow gullies and with its summit hidden; nor all that day was there anything more interesting in the way of land. But I did see an iceberg for the first time, though a small one; a fine sight, for it had a gentle slope running down to and no doubt far under the water, on which from time to time the long smooth swell broke tremendously. There were also whales, of more immediate interest, for we might be fishing in these waters in a few days; and we pushed on to Deception Island to get into touch with the fleet.

Day was just breaking as we hauled in for the entrance of the harbour. We seemed to be heading for a continuous wall of rock a thousand feet high when suddenly a narrow opening showed in it, so narrow that as we passed through it appeared as if a stone might fall on our decks from the crumbling cliffs that hung over our heads. The place was of an incredibly ferocious aspect in that cold twilight with the wind shrieking round the black pinnacles of lava that toppled on the skyline, but in a few minutes we had passed through the breach and opened up the vast harbour, a crater lake, in one corner of which was quite a little town; for Port Foster is an important whaling centre and during the season rivals Stanley in population. There were seven great steamers here moored along the beach, smoke rising from a factory on shore, whale-catchers and launches scurrying about, and millions of Cape pigeons and smaller petrels gorging on the refuse.

The whaling industry, of which I was to see a typical example (for the Tongans and Azoreans regard their whaling as a sport rather than an industry), depends nowadays entirely on good harbours lying near good fishing-grounds. The days when the South Seaman could make a living by cutting in his whales at sea, which means losing everything except the blubber, are gone; now every part of the whale goes into the pot, and to boil him down some hundred tons of fresh water are used daily by steamers of seven to ten thousand tons in their twelve boilers; or by an equivalent factory on shore. The floating factory, preferable so far South because able to avoid ice-bound areas, must be moored in a spot sufficiently sheltered to enable her men to cut up the whales from punts as they float alongside, and to handle the water-boats; and of course they have to be as near as possible to where the whales are killed, so they sometimes get into very queer places. Of which more

anon; just now we are being introduced to the gunner
or skipper of the catcher in which we are going out as
soon as she has coaled. These are wonderful little
vessels, fast, handy, and of necessity kept in perfect
order, for a chipped propeller, a loose rudder-head, or a
slack bearing would give the alarm as they steal on their
quarry. The art of getting even the handiest vessel of
some 110 feet length within twenty yards of a whale in
one of the brief moments when she comes up to blow is
to me a mystery, yet to the best gunners a whale sighted
is always a whale killed. I shall try to describe what it
looks like to a spectator, without trying to explain the
mental processes of the man who knows more about
whales than they do about themselves. We raise a spout,
perhaps a mile away. The whale usually blows two or
three times in quick succession before going down again
for ten minutes or so, thus one can judge in what direction she is travelling. The gunner steadies the helm and
then strolls off the bridge towards the gun platform. On
the foredeck he passes the lookout man, who has just
come down from the crow's-nest, and borrows a fill of
tobacco from him. The latter goes to the wheel, unless
there is already someone there. Meanwhile spectators
emerge from various parts of the ship.

When all these adjustments have been made the whale
blows again, right ahead, and a hundred yards away.
The helm is shifted a little and the engines rung slow,
the gunner looks for a convenient lee to light his pipe in,
then mounts the platform and casts loose the gun.
Nobody runs about or shouts, the few orders are given
in an undertone.

It seems an age of waiting till we see a vague greyness in the blue sea ahead of us. The helmsman gives a

little sheer to bring the target well out on the bow and expose her broadside; then the waters are parted and a flat head emerges; the great nostrils follow, throwing a jet of vapour into the air, and sink again. An interminable length of curved back rolls by, the gunner keeps his sights on the water-line, and not until half the whale has passed does he fire. And that is the end of her.

A huge hypodermic syringe is stuck into her and she is blown up with air, for whales killed thus would otherwise sink, and towed alongside by a strong chain passed round her tail, ready to let go if we want to be freed from our burden to chase another whale.

Of course it is not always so easy as this; in bad weather it must be very difficult to trace a whale's movements. Some whales, moreover, are perverse, and do not steer a steady course. Our second was an expert in the art of zigzagging, and it was some time before the gunner got the run of her manœuvres. In the end it was a lucky shot at extreme range that got us fast.

In the head of the harpoon is a bursting charge fired by a time fuse, and a well-aimed shot at close quarters will scatter scrap-iron all through the whale's vitals and kill her instantaneously. Our forlorn hope got home, but hardly crippled her, and she set off on the surface with the ship in tow.

Then we saw the wonderful gear that makes steam whaling possible. Between the harpoon and the winch the line is played by a tremendous battery of coiled springs fitted in the hold. Their effective extension is some thirty feet, through which the strain increases to fifteen tons, the limit of safety of the rope. With such fishing tackle the whale, once fast, has a poor chance. We hauled up alongside and gave her another shot that settled her. But that first harpoon had partly drawn and the air leaked out of the hole, so that we could not abandon her to go on other chases; accordingly we had to go home early and with no more than four or five hundred tons of booty; on our way we passed another catcher towing five whales.

All the interest of the game lies in the stalking; I should imagine that it requires more skill and knowledge to bring a steam vessel into position for discharging a gun with a limited arc of training than to get fast with a harpoon thrown in any direction from any one of three or four small boats.

The subsequent proceedings, after the catch is towed alongside the factory, are of interest only to the technologist; unless the cook has cut a piece of meat off the small. When I had tasted that as grilled steak I admitted that it was necessary to kill whales for the sake of the kitchen, though the other aspects of the industry rather disgusted me.

Apart from whales, the South Shetlands have no excuse for existing. They look all right on the chart; rather like the Outer Hebrides, for to seaward they are a mass of rocks and shoals, while towards the mainland they are steep-to and indented by deep sea-lochs which—or rather those of them that are not filled by glaciers—form good harbours. But the hills are of a rotten and recent black volcanic ash, of no beauty or grandeur; and the glaciation is altogether too complete to be tolerable. On a sunny day I might have enjoyed the great ice-falls round Admiralty Bay, and the huge séracs which seemed to be impending over the steamers moored there until I went aboard them, and then I saw that those cliffs were half a mile away and therefore, I suppose, 300 or 400 feet high. As it was, the whole landscape was an arrangement in dead and featureless white, black, and dull green, for the sea was so full of brash ice that it looked like pea soup; cold and infinitely depressing.

Deception Island is more horrible, but being a very recently extinct volcano still boasting a number of boiling springs it has a certain fascination. But the vapours from these springs, being discharged into freezing air, ruin the climate of the place completely; whenever I saw it, Deception was under a cloud. In spite of the abominable conditions I remarked some points of geological interest. Partly because of the very small catchment area and partly because the rocks are still warm, the glaciers are very small and one can see them shifting territory in a way that is not done in the Alps and that one cannot observe, if indeed it is done there, under a complete ice-sheet. Here the ice seems to plunge under a row of great pyramids of sand and cindery gravel, which, as they extend down the slope, become flatter until all merges into a smooth bank, that one would say was dry ground until one sees it cut off at the water's edge, and there the two materials are strangely intermingled. The ice is banded with lines of sand, in one place swelling in lenticular masses, in another dying out, and everywhere highly contorted and looking for all the world like a cliff of gneiss.

But what a depressing spectacle it all is! Round the gloomy lake stand as it were vast pit-head banks varied by patches of dirty snow, all black and white except where some reddish spikes stick up like ruined engine-houses built of cheap brick. You cannot see the clean snows of the heights, you cannot see the blue sky; a

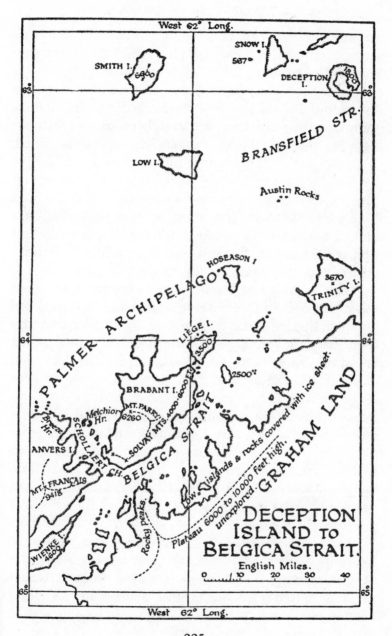

West 62° Long.

SNOW I.

567

SMITH I. 6800

DECEPTION I. 1800

63° 63°

BRANSFIELD STR.

LOW I.

Austin Rocks

PALMER ARCHIPELAGO

HOSEASON I

3670 TRINITY I.

64° 64°

LIÈGE I. 3500

BRABANT I. 2500

Melchior Hr. MT. PARRY 6260

Breeze Hr. SOLVAY MTS. 4000-6000 FT.

SCHOLLAERT CH. BELGICA STRAIT

ANVERS I.

MT. FRANÇAIS 9418

Rocky peaks

Low islands & rocks covered with ice sheet.

Plateau 6000 to 10000 feet high. unexplored GRAHAM LAND

WIENKE 4600

DECEPTION ISLAND to BELGICA STRAIT.

English Miles.

0   10   20   30   40

65° 65°

West 62° Long.

canopy of cloud presses down. You cannot look out on sunlight and colour, the breach in the walls is too narrow. It is a prison.

Such are all recently volcanic districts, but I was to see mountains of good old-established granite, mountains nine thousand feet high, and therefore, as they were between the 64th and 65th parallel, mountains of ice. I was to see ice compacting into glaciers, ice falling in ice-falls, ice forming lofty sea-cliffs, ice breaking off those cliffs into icebergs, and above all, the marvellous blue ice in the cavities of those floating hills which are only the remnant of the huge islands that have drifted up from the Antarctic. And I made certain observations on ice as it chiefly affects the mariner.

When I landed at Stanley the Collector of Customs asked me if I had seen Dougherty Island, at which I laughed, thinking that there was no such thing and that some iceberg had been reported as land. But now I know that one could not mistake an iceberg for land, it is far too fantastic a thing to be anything except itself. Anyone imagining an island would set the summit a little way in from the margin and make it slope down on every side, but the iceberg prefers to hang its summits (for it generally has two or more) out beyond its base; and of course no snow can cling to its overhanging faces which are therefore green, whereas if a peculiarly freakish island took the same shape, as is possible, they would be black.

It is easy to trace the evolution of an iceberg from the flat-topped square-cut section of the great Antarctic Barrier, through the crown between the points of which trickling water from the central depression is cutting notches, to the raft with towers set upon its edge; after that, anything may happen to it. Half the towers may drop off, and it will alter its trim and raise into view a long spur which had been submerged; it may split asunder, capsize, and expose water-worn bulbosities; it may lie on its side, divided vertically by the deep groove which the waves had cut round its previous water-line; it may melt quicker in the air, and rise; or quicker in the sea, and sink; it shows a dozen different planes of flotation and the scars of a score of cleavages; and every face, and facet, and crystal of it glows with a different colour. It must be seen to be believed, and even when seen can hardly be believed to have a material existence.

And I saw a thing which had even less material existence. As we approached the limit of the cloud-cap that grows like a mushroom out of Deception, an amazing vision leaped into the broadening belt of blue sky that lay along the horizon, a pile of frozen clouds borrowing all its delicate tints from the lately risen sun. Every fine day—and all days were fine—while we were in these waters that wonderful apparition hung in the sky over us. Now if it were really an island, as charted, with a latitude, a longitude, and a height of only 6,600 feet assigned to it, how could it be so ubiquitous?

Apart from these miraculous visits of Smith Island, the views in Bransfield Strait are not very attractive; one sees long snow-slopes rising from a singularly unpleasant rocky coast-line to peaks of an indeterminate height and distance, only one bold pyramid promising better things on a closer acquaintance. You cannot go closer on this, the dull side of the Palmer Archipelago; Nature has so protected it with shoals that you have to approach through Belgica Strait, and Belgica Strait is her masterpiece.

This deep-water channel runs for 30 miles inside a straight line of islands, Liège, Brabant, and Anvers, which lie so close together that no stranger could guess at navigable passages between them. Beyond it, to port, rises the colossal rampart of Graham Land, the Antarctic Continent, over I know not how many miles of level icefield, in cliffs 7,000 feet high, so steep that only an occasional glacier can cling to them; on the islands to starboard mountains no less lofty stand clear in separate peaks and ridges, hollowed by deep combes that pour out a tangle of séracs to fall into steep-walled sea-valleys; notched by snowy passes from which glaciers sweep smoothly to the water, there only wrinkled by the strain of giving birth to icebergs; and buttressed by dark rocky bluffs standing forward sheer into the channel. Down the middle of the strait extends a chain of rocks and small islands, which we leave on our port hand, for as we proceed they grow more continuous, and behind them lies only a blind alley into which no man has penetrated; but we can see through the narrowing passage and between the steepening cliffs away before us as far as the eye can reach; unless, indeed, it is blocked by ice.

All the place is full of ice, floating in, reflected in the glassy water; ahead and to starboard dazzling white on a pool of bright blue; astern and to port pale green against a sea of cream. No one that has only seen the crude colours of ice and snow and sky in the Alps could imagine how these are transmuted by the golden light of the sea-level atmosphere; even the rocks do not look black when veiled by the all-pervading luminous haze.

No one whose idea of snow peaks is 5,000 feet of white-wash on the top of 6,000 of ugly foothills could realize the completeness of this country where the lowest ground is a match for the highest mountains. And no one that has seen his mountains rising sheer out of the water wants to see them in any other way, unless he is a mere megalomaniac; for I admit that the Jungfrau seen from Interlaken is the tallest thing in the world—and the ugliest; and that here it was so difficult to give scale to the scenery that Mont Français seen from the Schollaert Channel did not look its nine thousand feet. And anyone who thinks that a glacier must degenerate into untidy heaps of muddy moraine will marvel at these ones, spotless from summit to where they break into sea-cliffs 300 feet high.

Though I saw all these mountains from sea-level I did not see them all from the sea, for the narrower part of the Straits was so full of ice, not only icebergs tabular and lately calved from near-by glaciers, or recently capsized and like mushrooms, or peaked like the Sgurr of Eigg, or coronate like water-lilies, but also floe ice, the frozen surface of the sea, that it looked like a very level glacier; but as no glacier is quite level, by the amount of its inclination do the mountains seen up it appear less steep than do those of Brabant and Anvers Islands.

We pushed carefully through to a spot which might have been the culmination of the mountain groups, the meeting-point of four great ridges; but which was in fact the meeting-point of three channels cut through the highest part of the system.

If one could be assured of access without too much trouble from ice in the two summer months, it would be

a perfect paradise for the mountaineer. The weather is so
uniformly calm that boatwork would present no difficulty; moreover there are sites, free from snow and other
obstructions (though the penguins have annexed the
best of them), on which permanent buildings could be
put in the shelter of aiguilles of red granite that would
not look out of place at Chamonix. No snow had fallen
for weeks when I was there, and the surface was in good
order for walking or ski-running; the glaciers move so
slowly that no avalanches ever fall nor do crevasses alter
their form or position. In fact the bolder spirits might
find mountaineering here rather tame; therefore, when
I am collecting an expedition to revisit the Southern
lands, I shall look out for six big-game hunters prepared
to man a whale boat. I have no scruples about killing
whales if I know that I can dispose of my catch; and
there is generally a factory in Melchior Harbour, some
ten miles away.

As soon as we turn to starboard down the Schollaert
Channel, towards Melchior and 'the open sea, an entirely different scenery is unfolded. The mountains stand
back from the shores on either hand, falling into gently
undulating slopes of unbroken snow, which are cut off
sharp and square in tremendous cliffs except where a
rocky pinnacle or spur divides them and affords a
means of access to their upper surface. The water
broadens, but is nearly lost in mazy passages between
islands of the same character as the shore; here and
there from them we can see smoke rising, or a mast
sticking up over the snowy ridges, where a factory ship
is lying. As we recede from them the great mountains
rise higher above low domes of snow; we shall see them
for a long time, for the land becomes always flatter and

the islands more numerous and smaller, till they are mere rocks entirely dominated by a huge flat berg 200 feet high and half a mile long which has grounded among them.

Then, dodging between these rocks, now so small and steep that no snow could lodge on them, we steered into Breeze Harbour, perhaps the most beautiful but certainly the most wildly improbable place that any captain ever took a 10,000 ton steamer into; a dream of golden granite rocks, blue water, and sparkling ice; but, one would say, more rocks and ice than water. This captain, however, does improbable things; wanting to ship a new propeller on one of his catchers he lifted her stern out of the water with his own derricks. Also he kills more whales than anyone else. But to-day there was trouble in Breeze Harbour; a big iceberg had drifted in and was threatening to pin his ship into a corner; this meant that she would have to clear out if or when her two catchers could shove that iceberg clear of her anchors, but as it weighed a thousand times more than they, their efforts were not conspicuously successful. However, her crew were all standing by, so that I was unable to go on a shore expedition with her doctor, as I had hoped, but had to take a short run along the coast in her launch until the turning tide helped the push-party to shift that iceberg. I chose the better part; a tramp over a vast and level snowfield I may enjoy—or the reverse—again; such an intimate acquaintance with icebergs in such a small compass I shall never have. We sported round them, we darted across them in a swirl of pale emerald water between their shining pinnacles; we squeezed between rocks, red, grey and yellow, and ice-cliffs white and blue, to my great alarm, for some of the latter were frightfully undermined at the water's edge and seemed tottering for a fall. And within the barriers of rocks and ice from a glassy pool rose crags of warm ruddy granite, populated by penguins and by graceful piebald cormorants with blue eyes and golden crests. I had often dreamed of this place, but thought it too wonderful to exist on earth. Perhaps it does not; perhaps I was looking at a bit of fairyland, and the fairies, to conceal the fact that I had discovered their secret haunts, had changed themselves to penguins. But I can make no certain observations on these matters; a mail steamer cannot carry a surveying and scientific expedition, and I had to go back from sunny, genial Anvers Island to cold and stormy Deception, and thence to Stanley; and it was really time that I thought about getting back to Dublin.

I saw M. married and paid off the ship; and three sheep killed, two for the harness cask and a third to hang in the mutton halliards; and being in all respects ready for sea and finding that the seal cruiser was going out early in the morning of the 28th of February, I tied up alongside of her to get as much as the weather would permit in the way of a tow.

CHAPTER X

SOUTH AMERICAN WATERS

On the 28th of February, therefore, I cleared for Ponta Delgada in the Western Islands, and as there is some dispute about the ownership of the Falkland Islands I went to the Consul to get a Portuguese bill of health. And that was about the only thing he could not do for me. He was consul for every country except Norway (who had one of her own), Argentina (who cannot have a consul in one of her own colonies), and, by mischance, Portugal. The incidence of consulates is very capricious; why should there be a Paraguayan but not an Uruguayan Consul at Auckland? I sailed with an Italian bill of health.

I felt very much comforted by the certainty, as far as one can be certain of anything about a maritime venture, after so many months of doubt, that I was going to bring my ship home. Previously, if the worst had come to the worst, and I had to abandon her in a port where she was unsaleable, I could have got myself sent home as a Distressed British Seaman, but with empty pockets, for I had not even an insurance policy on the yacht that I could raise money on. But now, as the difficulties of the voyage were passed one after another, my uninsured vessel began to appreciate in value, and I could talk about bottomry bonds without exciting derision. My agents in Ponta Delgada would surely see to it that a ship which had sailed 30,000 miles without

sustaining any damage should be in a position to sail
the remaining 1,300 to a place where she would acquire
an enhanced value. Or if I had to call at any port before the Western Islands, that port would be Pernambuco again, where my agents would know her worth.

These reflections were started by the memory that at
every port I had visited since Cape Town I had lost
one or more hands; I should have to call at some port
on my way home, and while I did not mind how many
hands I lost there, they might not get lost so cheaply as
at Melbourne and here. The one indeed whose loss
would be most desirable had a pay-day of over fifty
pounds coming to him, which he would hardly leave
behind, and I never succeeded in entering any port yet
with fifty pounds in cash on board. If I had I should not
press him to stay; if I could save even one month's
wages at fifteen pounds it would help the ultimate state
of my very shaky finances.

This ought to have been the easiest section of the voyage, and though I heard some grumbling about the
extra watchkeeping caused by M.'s defection, yet we
should soon be in the Trade Winds where no watch-
keeping was required. The first part was particularly
easy for the navigator; it did not matter if he got rather
to the North of his course, for he might expect plenty of
westerly wind to give him easting; it did not matter if
he got a great deal to the East, for he would pick up the
Trade Winds sooner, and they would be steadier and
more favourable. Were it not for this, standing through
the westerlies would be a troublesome job, for one is
cutting across the wind systems instead of travelling with
them, and in consequence one is sure of very changeable
weather.

When we sailed, the wind was, for the Falkland Islands, unexpectedly light and variable, with calms and fogs; during the first week there was only one day of a decent sailing breeze. I was now so near home that I was beginning to get anxious about the stories I should have to invent when I got there. The material was very scanty. I had seen no fabulous monsters, and I have rather a good eye for fabulous monsters; I saw the Lammergeyer in Switzerland in 1900 and the great sea serpent off the Kerry coast five years earlier. I had discovered no new lands; I sailed across a patch in the middle of the South Pacific marked "Shoal" on the chart, but I saw no shoal; small wonder, for the dotted line that defined it enclosed an area as big as Sussex. I was now very near a more authentic shoal, one with an acknowledged position and a name though with no depth assigned to it; and I intended, if the weather and the time of day suited, to get a cast of the lead on it and so, perhaps, my name into print. But I found that I was likely to be thereabouts at three o'clock in the morning, which is not a good time to approach unsounded rocks, and I did not want to spoil a good day's run by stopping to look for it—after all it was very small game—and I passed it by. I was 60 miles past it at noon on the 6th of March, when the look-out reported two patches of kelp ahead. I passed them by. I considered that I was 600 miles from land, out of the track of vessels, and had no boat; and that the prudent man would run down to leeward of them, and if he wanted to investigate work back cautiously rather than run over them with all kites set. I kept passing by patches of kelp for about an hour, and then I saw that a swell, which I had not noticed before, was getting up; and right ahead of us it ran into a tall pyramid, and I need not say I lost no time in altering course; and the next swell that came along was like a steep hipped roof and had a little crest of white on top; and the next was light brown in colour with a pale spot in the middle, and why it did not break I do not know, but I take no chances with blind rollers and was out of danger by that time. Now if anyone wants to take soundings within a cable's length of Saoirse Rock he had better wait for finer weather with less sea and swell than I had, for I doubt if there is three fathoms of water over it; and he will have to wait a mighty long time. I made the best of my way out of the neighbourhood. I did indeed pass over some kelp, but I could see no bottom below it, and kelp may grow in thirty fathoms of water. I wrote correctly on one page of my log-book that the latitude was 43° 21′ S. and the longitude uncertain, and on the opposite page incorrectly that the latitude was 40° 21′; and communicated the latter figure to the Hydrographer of the Navy. And thereby hangs a tale.

While I was at Stanley the Colonial Secretary had asked me to criticize a pamphlet published in Buenos Aires in support of the claim of that Government to the Falkland Islands in the matter of a statement that Sir John Hawkins never saw those Islands. (The whole seemed to me rather irrelevant, since Hawkins did not land and the English made no claim for 240 years and then by right of conquest, not discovery.) However, I was asked to give a professional opinion on the courses steered, winds and currents and so forth, and to reconstruct Hawkins' track on the chart, a thing too seldom done by the average commentator who occupies himself with textual minutiæ and would condemn an otherwise clear and consistent story for the sake of one printer's error. Now Hawkins said that he saw the land in the height of 48 degrees; and as there is no land there Hawkins is written down a liar, in spite of the fact that his own sailing-master—that is, the expert navigator, for in those days the captain was more of a soldier than of a sailor—gives the latitude correctly. So also Dampier and Cowley, sailing in the same expedition, on the same day saw the Islands in latitudes differing by three degrees. There seems to be a fog of inaccuracy over this part of the Atlantic even at the present day.

We had started off with a poor week's run, an average of only 124 miles a day, but the second week opened well though rather boisterously. After a night of good north-west breeze and moderate sea, the wind shifted to the South in a very heavy squall, and in an instant there was an amazingly steep high sea that swept the decks. It was so short that every wave was breaking, but it was not big enough to do any damage, so after I had stowed the mainsail and mizzen I found it quite pleasurable to watch the maddest turmoil of waters I have ever seen except in a tide-race. Before I got too chilly (for nothing would keep that water out, and even in 40° S. a southerly wind is never warm), the sea had lengthened out and we were running dry and easy again. This was a repetition on a small scale of my experience off Cape Leeuwin.

In the first four days of the week we did over 600 miles, and were in a good position, some 700 miles off the Brazilian coast, and with, I supposed (though the barometer was ominously high), ten degrees of latitude in which to expect westerly winds before I got the South-East Trade. The wind went round to the East at noon on the 11th of March, but I knew easterly winds did not last in 35° S.; it was light and the water smooth, and anyway I was on the meridian of Cape San Roque and could afford a more northerly course for a day or two. But next day there was more wind and more sea and the barometer was still higher and we were sailing slower; and it became most uncomfortably evident that we had hit a large anticyclone.

The textbooks give one explicit and in three cases out of four most practical directions for dealing with cyclonic systems and for picking a fair wind out of them; but nobody could deal with an anticyclone; it sits down in front of you immovable, unchanging; and this one was threatening to deal very unpleasantly with me. If I let it push me shorewards the wind would back continually till I got into the North-East Monsoon; and that's a fright. So instead of ramping away for Cape San Roque with all starboard stunsails set I was lying up as close into the wind as might be and pitching into an abominable head sea. Wind out of place, like any other matter, is dirt; this easterly wind in the region of the westerlies brought a dirty sea as well. I noticed that as soon as we got into the Tropics it became quite smooth; but in the meanwhile we were still 1,000 miles from the Tropics, with more than one hindrance in the way of getting there. Most serious was the fact that all our manoeuvres round the Falkland Island beaches had only resulted in cleaning one side of the ship, and of course it was the foul side which was to leeward, and dragging more heavily in the water. As the ship is a little slack on her helm on the starboard tack at the best of times, and as my best helmsman (if one can use the superlative of good in connexion with any of my helmsmen) had left me in Stanley, she was continually running off her course. Where, alas, was the prospect of all night which I had promised my crew and myself? And there seemed likely to be 3,000 miles of this kind of thing. After 600 of them I sent down the foreyard, which improved matters slightly. Then L., most unreasonably as I thought, after only a fortnight at sea, developed boils on his wrists of such severity that they incapacitated him, in his own opinion, at least, for heavy work. I considered that to wear oilskins continuously in that warm weather, however much spray was coming over, was asking for trouble; but I admit that I suffered pretty acutely though of course more transiently from sunburn. K. also had a fine boil on his elbow, but did not make any complaint about it. Why should I be so afflicted when I provide such variety of food and when K. cooks it so well?

I only suffered from depression caused by that odious wind and by the prospect of so many thousand miles more of it, and I need not have suffered so much had I known that I was only going to have a week of it, at least with that horrible sea attached; that I was going to make a good 840 miles on a correct course in that week, and that the other bad thousand miles, that is, the North-East Trades, was not going to be at all as bad as its reputation promised. Still, during that week I got to hate it. I hated in particular its music. Winds will produce surprisingly different results out of that orchestra which is a sailing vessel. Down in the Roaring Forties the great West Wind plays stately marches, solemn chords booming out, rising to a climax, and again falling, a sunrise put into sound. This East Wind, on the other hand, conducts his band in an irritating jerky style. He hammers out an obvious hornpipe rhythm with an eddy round the stern-post that sets the rudder shaking, and accents it with the blows of seas on the bow, while the wire stays squeal all up and down the scale as we pitch and scend, and every eighth bar or so is marked by a bang on the mainsail that resounds like a kettledrum. The ship seemed to like to dance to such music, but I was very glad when it was over for the time; when, on St. Patrick's Day, both the barometer and the sea went down and we had a little peace and comfort, though the wind had drawn a couple of points ahead. I had, however, now made the longitude I wanted, and was all right, if I could keep it.

On this day I saw a gannet, and he was a portent. I had seen plenty of albatrosses and petrels lately, but they are oceanic birds and may be met anywhere, but the gannet, I believe, goes home every night, and this meant that I was within his radius of action of the Ilha da Santissima Trinidada, and therefore, but for that confounded easterly wind, I should have completed the circumnavigation of the world. I was going to do so in three days at any rate, so I added to my armoury on the poop, which consisted of a harpoon and a rifle. For since I tasted whale steak in the South Shetlands I had been on the look-out for a porpoise, and to convert him into porpoise steak, which I suppose is just as good, I had acquired a harpoon in the Falkland Islands. Now I thought that few days would pass without their porpoise; I had even on one day suffered a plague of porpoises.

It happened this way. When I was going up from Auckland to Tonga I fell in with a school of porpoises, crossing my course at right angles. It was a pretty sight to see a score or so of them breaking out from the face of a wave simultaneously quite close aboard; it was amusing to see their antics and their struggles to dive again when they found the ship was in their way. After about half an hour they were coming thicker, they were, so to say, crowding each other at their fences, and some of them coming with an unpleasant whack into the vessel's side (for porpoises are not designed for end-on collisions like sperm whales). Lastly one of them, finding himself in a tight corner, jumped over my jib-boom. Now if any reader has the curiosity to consider my rigging plan he will see that in order to clear the boom and the bobstay and the back-ropes and the foot-ropes and the two jib down-hauls and the flying-jib sheets, an exceptionally agile porpoise was required. When I add that all this apparatus was alternately sweeping the troughs of the seas and scraping shreds off the clouds while the ship rolled along at eight knots, not one porpoise in a hundred would take the jump. And as the ship was rolling between upright and thirty-five degrees to leeward (for there was a big beam sea) and the weather back-rope was at times higher than the foot of the jib, I felt sure that the next porpoise that tried such tricks would go through that ancient and rotten sail. And as all gregarious animals tend to follow their leader, more of them would go through my newer but almost equally rotten mainsail; so I put up my helm and ran away before them, and if they tried any more high jumps they would only land in the chart-room or the galley (but I did not know then how good eating they were).

On this passage I had not seen one. The harpoon, however, did not stay all the time in its slings. There were one day a number of whales about, and as one rose along our quarter, K., who in spite of his city civilization had not entirely lost the instinct which all islanders have of going for a whale when they see her, no matter in what circumstances, hurled the harpoon at her. Fortunately in his excitement he forgot to cut the stop which held the coil of line, so he missed his shot and I did not lose my harpoon. I asked him how he proposed to kill a 70-foot finwhale with 40 fathoms of line intended only for porpoises; he thought it quite sufficient explanation that there was the whale and there was the harpoon and here was K. I wonder what the Pico ferry launch did when her crew (or passengers) met a whale, for she had no more line, and it was weaker. There are a great many mysteries in the sea, and none more strange than those concerning whales. How did sperm whales live through the centuries between the time when Science condemned Bishop Pontoppidan's account of the Kraken as a lie and the time when the Prince of Monaco proved that they could eat nothing but giant squid? How about that pseudo-science that rejected Jonah's story on the grounds that his whale could not swallow a herring? That day I saw a great extent of whale-feed, but it is a mighty thin soup for those that have to make an exclusive diet of it. Why does not the right whale go on to a fish course as the Rorquals do? Why should one believe anything that one has not seen oneself, or disbelieve anything at all?

I added to the harpoon and the rifle a stout fish-spear, a shark-hook, and a mutton-chop (I made a great mistake in putting the ribs of those poor little Falkland Island sheep into the harness-cask; in a month they were like leather, while the hams remained excellent), for I was now looking for a shark. I do not usually wish to have any dealings with that unsavoury monster; I did not want more of him than to recover my harpoon, spear, or hook, and cut off his tail, for this appendage I should be entitled to wear on my flying jib-boom as soon as I had circumnavigated the world. Alas! there were no more sharks than porpoises, or, for the matter of that, flying-fish, in the South Atlantic.

In view of this otherwise regrettable absence of sharks and of the fact that the sea was warm enough even for my taste, I ventured to bathe in what I consider the only perfect way, that is holding on to the bobstay, and thereby noticed how very even was the vessel's speed through the water with a good breeze, though on account of a considerable head sea she was really moving forward spasmodically; her 20 or 25 tons' weight counted for nothing. Hence if at the moment when she has no momentum she is struck by a cross sea or rolls all the wind out of her sails, she does not recover her speed and is carried bodily to leeward, so that to hold a good wind in rough water requires ceaseless vigilance on the part of the helmsman; a thing which I could not command and therefore did not try to realize. I was well content in these Atlantic Trades to make good 120 miles a day about six points off the wind.

Now at any moment I might come across the South-East Trade, as well as Trinidada and my outward track; and that outward track reminded me that the wind was so called not because it blew from the South-East but because it was easterly and blew South of the Equator; and easterly might mean anything between North-East and South-East, as eighteen months before it did; and I considered the Trade Winds, and especially this one, and sailing round the world in small and un-weatherly ships, which comes to the same thing. Both Captain Slocum and Captain Muhlhauser had gone with the sun, and with the Trade Winds, fearing, I sup-pose, as I also did, the long stretch of head winds and short steep seas which one must expect in one hemi-sphere or the other, going or coming. Not only small boat sailors went round this way, but also the early circumnavigators; perhaps through ignorance of the westerlies in the Southern Ocean, else how did Del Cano, bound from Manila to Cadiz, sight Amsterdam Island where an easterly wind occurs about once in a blue moon? Perhaps because they wanted to quiet their mutinous crews with Peruvian gold as soon as possible. But I know nothing of the navigational equipment of the earliest circumnavigator; I had better stick to the story of myself, who had just become the latest one.

I had passed Trinidada, I had passed my position of noon 558 days before, and I thought I had passed the South-East Trade Wind and fallen into the Doldrums. There was a tragedy about that Trade Wind; it got lost. So did the Doldrums, but that is another story. So did Trinidada, and that was so present a tragedy that I must say more about it. Of nearly all the places I had visited between Dublin and Deception, circumstances had pre-vented my seeing all that I should have, and I had them on my list for revisiting, knowing well that I should never do so. But I had deliberately passed Trinidada on my way out, to save time forsooth, because I was then a week behind my schedule date! knowing that I should see it properly on the way home. I saw it, and that was all; I saw it 30 miles away to windward of me (if there can be a windward when there is no wind), and if I could have got up to it I could not have landed, for though I had now a good boatman I had no boat. Never, dear reader, imagine that yachting is yachting in anything under a hundred tons with a brass-bound skipper and a dozen of a crew.

I was now virtually reduced to one of a crew. For some time past I had noticed that K. was doing most of the work of the ship, and though he did not complain of it I did. It was no good. L. complained of a weakness, and was in fact becoming a complete passenger. It was still over 3,000 miles to the Western Islands in a straight line, and what with non-existent South-East Trades and too strong North-East Trades and goodness knows how many miles of Doldrums in between, I decided that he should be a passenger to the nearest port, and no farther; and altered course for Pernambuco, as I had done once before with trouble on board. But this time the trouble would hit me lightly, for L. and I would part by mutual consent, which meant that the Consul and not I would find him a passage home.

We brought the wind well aft, what there was of it, and sent up the foreyard and set the foresail and the foretopsail and the starboard lower stunsail and the mizzen-staysail, making with the working canvas, the flying-jib, jib, mainsail, gaff-topsail and mizzen, nine sails in all, and when I saw K. spreading blankets upon boat-hooks I thought he was setting a tenth; but no, he said, he was only drying them. I think if they had been a little whiter he would have admitted they were helping the ship along.

We were an unconscionable time getting up to our port, and the wind was either right aft or all round the compass, which meant continual shifting of the foretopsail and stunsail, for we had only one of each, or, I should say, the stunsail was what might otherwise have been the lee foretopsail (which would be blanketed by the gaff-topsail if the fore-and-afters were set) borrowed for a more useful purpose. Lastly came heavy showers of rain and squalls, between which I struggled to get the foresail unbent and stowed away dry, for we should not want it for three weeks or more, and as the book said this was the rainy season at Pernambuco I could not make sure of drying it there. But I crossed the foreyard again and set the topsails over it, and we must have astonished the natives by our rig as we came up the coast very close inshore, for all their small craft are pure fore-and-afters.

We had made a bad landfall at Cabo Agostinho, some 15 miles too far South; but K. was delighted with this, for he was seeing palm-trees again and hearing the boom of the breakers on the reef after eight months and anxiously speculating as to whether yams were obtainable in Brazil. My interest in this reef, which extends nearly continuously and forms a safe narrow canal along 500 miles of coast, was solely that the next opening in it formed the harbour of Pernambuco, "Recife," "the Reef" *par excellence*. I do not much admire palm-trees in bulk, though a few well-grown ones are an ornament; still they were trees, and that I had not seen for five months. But what I was looking out for was a sign of civilization, a building with some definite style about it. I rejoiced in the Church of Nossa Senhora dos Praseres, though there is nothing duller or more conventional than a Portuguese church, inside or out; and where you see a dozen in one little village as at Olinda, it suggests a toy-shop; and when I opened up the city I thought how well one does to go to the other side of the world in order to appreciate how much better things are done on this side. When I first saw Pernambuco I compared it with the cities of Europe; now the last cities I had seen were in Australasia.

I say nothing here against Colonials as such, but they descend from Northerners, and no Northerner can build a town. To him his house is his castle, and he may build it where and how he likes. Whether the Brazilian architect is censored by the Town Council, or whether he is influenced by the traditions of the spacious times when Emperors planned and laid out whole cities, he builds not rows of houses but streets, not bunches of tenements but towns. We do not even care for what amenities we have; we could not set a little square in the busiest part of a city of a quarter of a million souls and plant it with grass and flowers and trees, with never a railing nor a notice-board. In Brazil even small boys do not scribble on blank walls; even big shops use discretion in their advertisements.

Because he orders his streets and squares and the skyline of the houses, the architect here may without offence let himself go over the detail; and he generally does. I see no absolutely good nor absolutely bad styles; if something rather rococo suits the environment, it may give more pleasure than the severest classic. And I am sure the owner gets more amusement, and does less harm, by decorating a well-designed house, than by designing a house which Academicians will have to try to save by decoration. This matter of towns is not geographical; it is Rome against the barbarians, not South against North, though the most southerly town in the world, Punta Arenas, is as beautiful and as typical as any in South America—and I have no doubt that its streets are as cold and as draughty as those of the New Town of Edinburgh.

By now I knew enough about pilots to waste no time getting into the harbour; and I came in with more style too; both foretopsails set as we rounded the breakwater, so that I was afraid we might not be recognized as the same vessel that crawled in before under close-reefed mainsail. However, they are better at distinguishing flags here than in New Zealand; the pilot met me at the top of the Poço and signalled to me when to anchor; and the doctor, customs, and police merely paid a formal call. The latter indeed asked what I had been doing during the past year and a half; his cousin owns a news-paper and he is its Shipping Reporter. I need hardly say that I had two columns and half a page of pictures in the next issue, though I grieve to state that he still had not got my nationality right and located Dublin somewhere in England. Meanwhile my agent's launch had come alongside (there was no doubt that I had been recognized while I was outside the breakwater, for I was not expected on this or any other day) to take me ashore.

I have written, on the authority of the *South American Pilot,* that this was the rainy season, and it was late in the evening when I tried to get to the office through a procession of I do not know how many scores of statues and shrines or how many thousands of people that had been occupying four or five miles of the streets all day; and at that late hour it did not look noticeably the worse for the weather, except that the starch had run out of some of the angels' wings. So much for the rainy season.

Statistics give an average fall of a quarter of an inch a day at this time of the year, but statistics also allege a South-East Trade; in a word, they lie. Only alternate days are showery and then mostly at night; and one's clothes dry as soon as the rain stops. Where it is nice and warm this cannot be called a bad climate.

Next morning I towed up to my old berth opposite a new quay which, as well as testifying to the prosperity of Pernambuco, indicated that the dredgers had stopped working in that part of the river and therefore I might expect a quieter anchorage than I had before. But another sign of the prosperity of the place was that in spite of the new quays the trade was outrunning the capacity of the river. I call it a river, as anyone would who has pulled a boat up it after heavy rain in the country, but it is really two miles of the natural canal behind the Recife widened and deepened by the scour of the two rivers: Capibaribe, which flows in two wide branches through the city and presents unexpectedly at the end of every street an excuse for a fine bridge, a mirror for noble buildings, or a picturesque tangle of barcaços and coasting schooners; and Bebaribe, whose vast waters roll muddily between palm-crested sand-banks down from the Great Unknown. Previously my only trouble, apart from the dredgers, had been with lighters that had broken adrift; in that current two 50-ton lighters lashed together saddle-bagged across one's hawse are no joke. Now there were so many craft in the river that we were all more or less in foul berths, and generally half a dozen of us foul of each other every time the tide turned. But a providential barquentine came down from Nova Scotia and scattered the smaller fry to an even more congested anchorage; and I tied up alongside the barquentine, for I knew the local boats would take care to keep clear of her, and I had to wait a week before I got on to the patent slip, which had now been reinstated.

The owners of the slip hauled me up and launched me for (they said) the price of the labour, but unless labour got something less than sixpence a day, and then did not charge for scrubbing and painting, this was only a token. The pilots charged me nothing; my light dues were remitted; only that horrid tribe who live by defacing revenue stamps, people who do nothing for me or for anyone else, made me pay for their infernal stamps, and their time spent sticking them on, and their ink and interest and depreciation on their fountain pens; as it is all over this degenerate world, where the man with the plough, the hammer, or the marling-spike is too generous to survive in a generation of Shylocks. But, lest I flatter unduly, let me qualify this generosity of the Brazilian by suggesting that out of the excess of their prosperity they treated me so well. I know nothing of the implications of Foreign Exchanges, and doubt if they have any; last time I was here I hardly saw an aluminium-bronze milreis; now as like as not I got a handful of silver in my change. And where else do people put gold-leaf on the funnels of their steamers?

In another way Pernambuco revisited was not quite the same. It appeared, as one sees things during a partial eclipse of the sun, and as I see places in a dream, never to be quite in full light; moreover objects, like the wares in the Looking-Glass Shop, had a way of turning into something else or of vanishing altogether if I gazed hard at them. I supposed that the cooler air on the water, green spectacles, and a couple of days' rest would put me right again and did not regard it as a seriously un-favourable omen. Otherwise everything was propitious; and I told the despatchers to get my clearance for Dublin made out for the 6th of April.

CHAPTER XI

THE RETURN

THE voyage which I began on the 7th of April (for the despatchers were too busy speculating in Ford cars, which were at that time being imported at the rate of 150 a week, to let me have my papers early enough to sail the day before) was not part of my cruise round the world; I was merely going on a yachting trip to Dublin, and I took the affair about as seriously as one usually does take yachting trips; very differently from my anxious departure from this port 19 months before.

There was more than the difference between an outward and a homeward, a south-going and a north-going, an experimental and a proved voyage. Then I had already had trouble with my crew, and left in a bad temper with things in general; now K., promoted mate, for whom I had as much respect and affection as he for me, smoothed my way through all. I never had any doubt that he would be satisfied with a ship's company of two; the only thing I was afraid of was lest the Consul should want to send any distressed British Seamen home with me. (Are there no laws, you ask, respecting the undermanning of vessels? Not of yachts.) However, that peril was averted and I was so sure this was going to be a happy and comfortable passage that I started keeping a diary to tell the world how I felt about it; an occupation most detrimental to sound history. For if one refrains from thinking of, or at least writing of, facts for a decent interval one can present them with reference to the world at large; but the diarist gets his facts confused with emotions and personalities which are of no permanent interest, but which tinge their significance and distort their truth. Even if a diary is destroyed the evil that it does lives after it; the record of this voyage from Pernambuco as far as the Western Islands therefore must not be believed so implicitly as the others which I have made.

I did not realize at all how bad my sight was till the ship had been towed (of course it was a free tow) outside the Great Passage and was lying up close-hauled between the Olinda Reef and the English Bank, with the usual early morning light wind and lumpy sea. I could see the churches on Olinda Point, for they were uncomfortably close; I could see the breakers on the reef, for they were closer still; but for the life of me I could not see the buoys that mark the channel, nor tell from the chart how many they were nor of what shape or colour. I had hopes of a barcaço that went out ahead of us, for a guide, but she went inside the reef, and that was not for us. In such a case the wise man makes a tack, no matter who is looking on; the proud man thinks of what the pilots are saying; and the fool hits the reef. I was proud without being foolishly so—or rather without being excessively foolish, for it is mere folly to waste one's labour in showy seamanship; nowadays if it comes off everyone assumes that you have a motor; and they are generally right, because the kind of seaman that could carry through a smart manœuvre is now nearly extinct.

No one can expect too much of a Trade Wind, or indeed of any kind of wind, close to the land, so I was not disappointed when I found it very light. As the sea, outside Recife roads, which is one of the most disagreeable places in the world, was smooth, this was a day for a multitude of small jobs. Both Primus stoves were out of order, and I had no spares; we breakfasted on sardines, bread and cheese, and white wine; very nice, but not breakfast. It is true that we had half a ton of good coal on board, but we did not want to use it in this weather. One seldom feels oppressive heat at sea, but in the absence of that unmentionable Trade Wind we did so now; and curiously K. felt it worst. But then he wore more clothes; to prevent sunburn, he said, but I suspect because his English grandfather was a Methodist, for he told me that my costume would only pass in a German sphere of influence—by which I presume he meant Samoa. Both sextants were unusable, my own I hoped only temporarily indisposed—I had better say something about sextants.

Since the mate I shipped at Melbourne had none and I thought it very immoral to go to sea without a second for fear of accidents, I bought one for the ship. I picked it out from a good many because it had the clearest engraving on the arc, and wrong reading is the commonest cause of wrong navigation in a small vessel. The shopman sandpapered all the divisions off before he sent it down to me; at present, anyway, it was useless. My own had a wet swab put down on top of it by one of my late crew, and the silvering had come off the horizon glass. I took it to the tailor's shop in Pernambuco where I had bought my flags on my first visit to ask the chronometrista to resilver it; but unfortunately the chronometrista had disappeared, whether eaten by his rattlesnakes or not I did not learn. I went to another shop owned indeed by an honest man but staffed by young know-alls who cut up a shaving glass and substituted a piece of it for my plane mirror; so that one saw two or more suns of different shapes and sizes in it. The owner of the shop, attracted no doubt by my language, came on the scene and relieved the strain on my French vocabulary, which was my only medium for profanity, in Portuguese, and when that ran dry in Norwegian and the language of the United States of North America, recovered my glass and promised to get it re-silvered and sent off by the tug-master who was to take me out in the morning. But I, fearing a miscarriage, took the sextant, as if necessary I might be able to fit one of the glasses out of the other instrument. The replacing of the proper glass would not have been an easy job in my state of blindness, but repeated experiments with the shaving glass had evidently ruined the tiny clips and screws which should secure it, and I lashed it with a bit of sail-twine.

And so I got (as I supposed) one good sextant, but there was only one very indifferent navigator to use it. However, as my eyes were improving, I postponed teaching the art to K. until we got on the same side of the Equator as the Sun, to avoid a multiplicity of rules; in a boat with only one companion it is more important to teach him piquet.

On the third night out we kept rather perfunctory watches, lest we should hit Fernando Noronha, but as a matter of fact we passed well to the eastward of it, though not far enough to be on our proper course. K. told me, when I came on deck in the morning, that he could see from the masthead steamers passing to starboard; the evening before they had passed to port. It was our bad steering, not theirs; already in $3\frac{1}{2}°$ S. the wind was heading us. Now K. was not aloft at six o'clock in the morning in order to look at the shipping, but to grease down the spar and put fresh seizings on the ratlines; I should like to see some of those good people who say Polynesians are lazy do as much. And next morning (it had been a clock calm night and I had taken in the kites and sheeted the rest flat amidships to save chafe) he was on deck first and had all sail set and drawing before I woke up. Now only one of all my other hands would have set that gaff-topsail, and only two would even have trimmed the sheets if I had not been there to tell them to do it. It was an ill day when K. advertised his accomplishments as cook. And yet I do not know whether a good cook is not more necessary to a small vessel than a good mate; without the latter you may arrive at your journey's end late, but without the former you may not arrive at all. The principal thing on a long voyage is to keep oneself alive and one's ship afloat, and let her drift around on whatever wind the good God thinks best for one; so I will use no more hard words about this alleged Trade Wind, at least in my own regard.

I do not think it is playing fair to the birds and butterflies of this district, however. They are accustomed to lean up against it, as the native of Wellington leans up against his local air; and just as the Wellingtonians fall down every time they walk round a street corner in Auckland, so when the Trade Wind is unexpectedly withdrawn butterflies fall out into mid-Atlantic; else why should a fine big fellow come alongside this day, 140 miles from the nearest land?

My noon sights on the seventh day out—what a time

to take from Pernambuco!—indicated that we had somehow drifted across the Equator a little to the west-ward of the Penhedo de São Pedro, which you may also call the Rocks of St. Paul. But why you may so call them I do not know. I can understand that the Netherlands should be Dutch, and the Dutch German, for it is all in the family; I can understand Erse, which means Scot-tish as opposed to Irish Gaelic, being used in the ex-actly opposite sense by people who carefully cultivate an ignorance of these subjects; but why St. Peter should become St. Paul (or *vice versa*) passes my comprehension. But the names of places and people have an amazing attraction for inaccuracies; which is the more unfortu-nate in that an arbitrary spelling mispronounced by a railway porter may destroy a page of unwritten history. In view of which it is, I think, not pedantic of us in Ireland to transcribe these names into a standard spel-ling, as the Scots and Welsh have done, before they be-come hopelessly corrupt. So for the second time I crossed the Equator, and K. was a very much more travelled person and therefore Neptune did not pay us his customary visit. And here, just to show that I was wrong in stating that the South-East Trade blows South of the Line, it tried to make amends in eighteen hours for as many days of defection.

The one merit of a properly kept diary is that one can satisfy oneself, if the result proves it desirable, that a prophecy was really a prophecy and not a memory in-spired by events. I wrote this evening, "We shall both be able to turn in all night again with the certainty of finding the ship on her course when we wake up in the morning." Why I should have written this I do not know, for as far as I can remember it was assumed on all but two of the twenty-eight nights we spent on this passage; unless it was a piece of bravado addressed to my subconscious and more truly prophetic soul which warned me that a change of weather was not far off. I did not justify or otherwise comment on my taking in the light canvas and waking an hour earlier than usual.

At six next morning I called K. to look at the North-East Trade; and by God it was worth looking at. The water, which had held a pleasant ripple all the night, grew inky black to windward; partly from the premonitory ruffling of the breeze, and partly from the reflection of the cloud which brought it; and dazzling white by contrast, heavens high above it, stretched a line of foam, bellowing as only a distant squall can across two miles of calm. Nothing, I thought, but a torrent of rain could cause such hissing and roaring of waters, so it was not necessary to postulate a great deal of wind as well. So I kept the ship off a couple of points to have plenty of way on her, and waited for the rather alarming apparition to come along. It was really only by contrast, by analogy, by anything except inherent frightfulness that it was alarming. The contrast of what looked like a different element being poured over the smooth water to which we had been accustomed was strange; the analogy, as far as distant appearance went, with a Severn bore, promised trouble. Curiously enough both of us looked only at the sea, which was almost entirely an optical illusion, and not at the wind, which was quite considerable. The ship took it on her beam, for so she was on her course for Dublin (and if anyone cares to work out this course he will see that the North-East Trade is sometimes no more northerly than the South-East Trade is southerly). She went from her

sober five knots in one jump to eight, and then—I have
an authentic record that she once did ten in similar
circumstances at home; ten, that is, measured on a
measured mile and checked by a patent log; and I do
not suppose she was doing less to-day. But it could not
last; continuous cataracts were coming over both bows;
the weather one shooting up the mainsail and streaming
off the peak of the gaff; to leeward it was the Atlantic
Ocean, and that tried to find its own level, which was
generally about that of the topgallant rail, till it was
scooped up into the air by the break of the poop and
whirled away like a miniature waterspout in the lee of
the mizzen. When the sea got up I should start losing
things if I did not take the bonnet off the mainsail; so
reluctantly I put up my helm and reduced canvas as
quickly as I could, for I did not want to run farther than
was necessary in the direction of America; I had, I supposed, 1,600 miles before me during which I should be
continually driven too far westward.

I was rather surprised that when I told my sailmaker
in Auckland to make a bonnet for that mainsail he
knew what I was talking about, but he was a very old
man; for the benefit of the generation that has never
seen that article I will explain its nature. This heavy-
weather mainsail was made the size of an ordinary mainsail with a reef in it; the bonnet is a strip of canvas the
depth of the reef which is laced on to the foot of the sail.
When one is likely to be under reduced canvas for a
week at a time it is a great advantage not to have to
carry a bag of water or possibly ice in the rolled-up reef.

Here if the Trade was blowing fresh I found the best
rig was "reef and topsail," as they call it at Brixham;
and this day the gaff-topsail was very soon set, for the

wind took off, though naturally it backed more northerly, and there was never much sea. So we made a
good enough course, sometimes at 5 knots, sometimes
at 6, but what actually were the course and speed for
the next four days (or indeed at any time since leaving
Pernambuco) I do not know; and this is why.

One day I was instructing K. in winds and currents,
and I said: "Here is the Equatorial Current; this morning we shall find ourselves 60 miles farther West than
we expect." And it was so. But in the afternoon I took
other sights, and it was not so, at all. A whole degree,
60 miles, is an error that should not be made by a careful navigator. I thought the lashing on my sextant must
have come adrift, but that was tight. I pointed the instrument at the horizon, and the horizon was continuous; I pointed it at the sun, and with a click one sun
became two. Those shop-boys had tampered with the
index glass too, for how could a screw which had not
been touched for ten years become as loose as that?
What wonder that I call on the Devil to provide special
accommodation for them? I fixed this up with a small
wedge of hard wood; the instrument worked all right,
but looked fitter for a museum specimen than an aid to
practical navigation.

So I cannot say if the Equatorial Current runs 30
miles a day, or not at all and is, like the South-East
Trade, the Doldrums, the Sargasso Sea, and the Horse
Latitudes, all of which I offered, and failed, to demonstrate to K., a myth. He said that we had Doldrums in
the South-East Trade, and that they manage these
things better in the Pacific; against which I quoted
Captain Muhlhauser's very unpleasant experiences between Papeete and Suva. And whatever he said about

the Southern Hemisphere I would cheerfully challenge
him or any other islander to show me better weather
conditions, for our particular needs, than we were getting in the North Atlantic. Here we were doing our five
knots on a bowline—I am fond of that phrase, for it is
just suitably vague; if I said "close-hauled" or "by the
wind" someone would point out that I was heading
N.N.W. and therefore, with my rig, implied that the
wind was N.E. by N.; which it wasn't, not by a point or
more. I sail "full and by," with the emphasis on the first
word; or "on a wind," which is the vaguest of all; but
by preference on such a course as I could steer with the
foreyard braced sharp up and the bowline, which leads
to the end of the flying jib-boom, keeping the weather
leach as taut as I can make it; or, to put it into figures,
not much less than six points off the wind. But now, and
nearly always, the foreyard being down on deck, the
expression is merely figurative, as it is also to those many
ships that do not use bowlines. In fact all these phrases
only mean getting to windward as seems to the men-
tality of each captain best for the capabilities of his ship,
and sailing on a bowline seems best to me—for the most
part under the five lowers with the gaff-topsail over the
small mainsail. Though this would be a heresy in the
Solent, I believe in keeping the sails low at sea, for high
up they lose their efficiency, through the exaggeration of
rolling and pitching, and in spreading them out fore-
and-aft, which makes a vessel steadier on her helm. So
my flying-jib, which for long ranked as an ornament of
such delicate texture that it could only be used in calms,
is now, much patched and mended, one of the working
sails, and does not come in till there is a reef in the mainsail.

From a practical point of view the North-East Trade could not have done better for us, but it was infinitely tedious. I was reduced to making futile observations such as: "To-night I saw the North Pole Star." It is the one alleviation of this northerly course that the constellations are coming right side up, and it is surprising how quickly they change, and that makes one feel nearer home. Otherwise one is plagued with the fast-changing climate and weather; it was nice and warm now, but we should be out of the Tropics in a week, and after that might be trying the worst the North Atlantic can do for one in the month of April. A more interesting observation was that we had flying-fish for breakfast, for I had not even seen any since we left Nukualofa. But they are birds of ill-omen; when they fall on deck it is a sign of more wind and sea than I want; so much so that for the first time deliberately with that purpose I hauled the ship up close and by and left her head-reaching so as to facilitate dinner. That is to say, I steered four instead of six points off the wind, making, I suppose, 2½ knots instead of 5. It is the pace that kills men as well as glassware, and a couple of hours' peace and quiet are wonderfully refreshing, much more so in this short sea than in the Roaring Forties where the rhythm of motion is more varied.

All things come to an end, and after eleven days and 1,320 miles of the North-East Trade (which is not too bad going) in lat. 23° N. and long. 38° W. (nor is that out of the way) the wind went round to South and then South-West, though very light. We sent up the foreyard, set all square canvas, and crossed the Tropic of Cancer; and later for the first time in seven weeks at sea had the wind on the port side, and felt it very strange. It is disconcerting to put out a hand to steady oneself by a familiar rope or spar, and find that it is not there; it might have been dangerous but that I had rigged waist-high lifelines on both sides at Stanley. Why I had waited to do this until I was practically home, instead of doing it before rounding the Horn, was because until I went to the West Falklands in the Government Cruiser I did not know the proper way to rig lifelines. Commonly, if the boat lurches over so far as to throw you against the lines, you pull the stanchions out, and all goes overboard together; so I reckoned I was safer without them; but when I saw that if you bend the stanchions inboard you are not thrown so far and in any case cannot pull them out, I made two sets to show those who knew no more about safety in small yachts than I had just before how that quality may be attained.

Though there was the most immense swell that I have ever seen rolling up on our port beam and the winds were rather light and variable, we could keep all our canvas full and drawing and did not expect any interruption in a comfortable and pleasant passage, when K. reported sick and thought he was going to die; and after consulting my medical book I thought so too. It was the fault of my eyes and of the small print that I fell into this mistake, and when after four days he was still alive I felt that I must have made a wrong diagnosis; but by that time I could not read any print. I should have thought about nothing but my navigation, which was all I could do to get the ship along, for we were nearly 1,000 miles from anywhere; but I forgot that I had come out here for a rest-cure and worried myself into such a state of blindness that I ran considerable risk of missing the Western Islands altogether.

But three days of a 6-knot breeze brought me within hail of a passing Japanese steamer, who confirmed my position; and next morning I woke to find the huge cone of Pico hanging over my head; and you will say that it would be hard to miss Pico which is 7,500 feet high; and I tell you that Pico is for three-quarters of the time in the clouds and it was very obliging of him to be clear on the morning of this 5th of May. As we drew nearer, the wind fell to a calm through which the long unfamiliar rattle of the surf on a stony beach came loudly; and as we drifted along the sound of church bells ringing the Angelus; and, for the tide was almost done, most welcome of all, the chugging of a motor-launch that had seen my signals of distress. And the owner of that launch was a decent man and did not read into those two flags their ordinary meaning, "You may charge me what you like for your services," but towed me into the harbour of Horta for a very small sum, where the ship was tied up to a Government buoy and I, after seeing K. to the hospital, sat down to complete my interrupted rest-cure.

The island of Fayal, and all the others except Santa Maria, which alone is a remnant of the old continent, occupy part of the site of Atlantis, but are the product of later volcanoes. Like many other volcanic islands they come and go; the last came in 1811 and went in 1812; and even the more permanent in position are not always permanent in shape. Of that I was reminded by the ceremony which I saw on Whit-Sunday, by which the City expiates a vow to provide a meal for the poor if the flow of lava that threatened Praya do Norte stopped. It was laid out on tables running the whole length of the main street, at the top of which stood the memorial chapel, from which came three old men in long scarlet gowns; and the first was beating a tabor, and the second a triangle, but the third, because he was very old indeed, was walking with a stick; and they recited to a queer barbaric chant the history of the eruption. A priest followed them, blessing the meal; and as soon as he had gone small boys went in and rummaging behind the altar produced large bundles of rockets which they let off indiscriminately, while several bands played different tunes, and wherever there was space enough to do so without killing anyone land mines were sprung. This is good, healthy, unselfconscious religion, strange to our respectable and sect-ridden country.

Some at least of these islands are of a respectable antiquity; Corvo had a trade with Carthage, and I am by no means sure that the Milesians did not come from them; and some people even say all Western civilization. Certainly the architecture of Fayal has considerable affinities with that of Ireland, which is so unlike either the Northern or the Roman styles. But from the appearance of the people one can tell nothing of their origin, for in this island they are heavily crossed with the Flemish.

The signs of this are on their house-fronts. Just as at Pernambuco, which was once a Dutch Colony, these are covered with small tiles, sometimes a chequer work of two colours, but more often white with the same pattern on each, which produce a handsome effect but have, by requiring large flat surfaces, killed the older manner of building with bold bases, strings, and cornices of stone. But the finest collection of tiles in Fayal, if not in the world (though a church at Pernambuco runs it close) is in the chapel of Nossa Senhora da Guia, which had another origin. Three Dutch ships were out of their reckoning in a heavy gale, and the Commodore vowed a chapel to Our Lady on the first land he saw. And he had to build it on the lip of the steepest little volcano you ever met, hanging over a crater at the bottom of which (for one side is knocked out) is a pool of the sea 300 yards across. They did not go into that, for the entrance is too narrow, but round the corner into Horta Bay; as many vessels have done since, and lastly mine; and if there is any trouble about my offering to Our Lady of Limerick, it shall go to Our Lady of Guidance at Fayal. And when they had built the chapel to her they put the story of their miraculous delivery on the front of the altar, and round the body of the chapel a landscape of the period diversified with very tall and ruinous temples and porticoes, among which walked very small gentlemen in steeple hats and plus fours, talking to Adam and Eve or the Christian Virtues or whoever it may be, all in blue tiles; but in the sanctuary separate tiles, each with a picture; one series windmills and drawbridges, another small craft with the various rigs of the seventeenth century, birds, flowers, fishes, and, most amusing of all, whales; a fearsome gallery of impossible monsters.

This chapel is now only used by whale-men; once a year for their feast-day, and the rest of the time as their look-out place; for whaling is, after football, the national sport, and a man sits up here, 500 feet above the sea, all day in the season looking out for spouts. But while I was here he saw none; a sad disappointment, for the Pico boats killed two sperm whales, but of course I could not get out to them in time. As in the old days when these things were done commercially American whalers used to call here for harpooners, Fayal is very

distinctly the next parish to New Bedford, and in fact
has contributed largely to the population of the latter
place. I was therefore not surprised to see that two
locally built schooners—the Pico farmers who built and
manned them are also an enterprising people—were,
in hull design, copies of the Gloucester fishermen, and
the latest type at that, the racing fisherman. Consequently, though they were twice the size of my ship, I do
not think they would carry very much more cargo than
I could. Evidently freighting, like whaling, is regarded
primarily as a sport. They were rigged with very tall
narrow sails, nearly of a size, but the larger forward,
peaked very high, and with no topsails; an ugly rig and
the new stiff canvas set very badly in light weather, but
the weather round these islands generally exceeds in
the other direction, and no doubt they would look better with a reef or two tied down.

Naturally this island was full of good seamen, and
several wanted a passage with me; but nowadays the
immigration laws make such casual engagements
troublesome and expensive, so as, although K. was now
quite well, I felt my self-sufficiency rather shaken, I had
asked my sister to come out and see me safe home.
When she came I rashly appointed the 1st of June for
sailing, and communicated this to Dublin; whereupon
my friends there appointed the twentieth for my arrival,
and for the holding of a great reception, and communicated that not only to me but to the Press of the world.

I had not realized how holidays flow over from one
week to another, nor that this one was the big event of
the Fayal year. We got away on the third, and then only
by sailing out of the harbour and standing off and on in
the roads while my agent chased around for papers.

Still, seventeen days for 1,300 miles should be ample allowance, and as we ran before a steady breeze up Fayal Channel we were speculating as to where we should spend that week which we thought we should have to pass in hiding till the day of the reception.

It is true that the wind soon dropped to the lightest of northerly airs, but that I discount near islands, and we were cheered by dropping a big schooner far astern. But on the fifth a good South wind blew up, and though another, a medium-sized schooner, passed us, I did not mind, for we were doing 7 knots if he was doing 10; anyway, it was a pleasant change to get into waters just moderately crowded with shipping. But the pleasantest thought was that all the indications of wind and barometer were those of a cyclonic system travelling towards Ireland at exactly our speed, which should bring us straight to the Tuskar without touching the wheel or any rope.

With three cable companies and an observatory at my hand, and a particularly smart navigator in my agent's office, it was pure folly not to have made some inquiries about the state of the weather ahead of me. If I had any indication of the anticyclone into which I ran after three days of that good wind—and anticyclones alter so slowly that it would have been probable —I should, or perhaps I ought to, for I sometimes sin against the light, have kept well to the westward of it and come in by the North Channel, in which, I believe, there was plenty of wind at the time. Even when I did strike it, right in the middle, this would have been the better course; but one cannot refer any chance calm or easterly wind to an anticyclone on only one day's observation. So being only some 350 miles from the Fastnet, and well in the way of traffic, we kept on, hoping before long to signal some homeward-bound vessel, or the lighthouse, and report our progress to the organizers of the reception. And this day, the ninth of June, was calm with fog.

And the tenth was calm with fog, but whatever wind there was came from the E.N.E.

And the eleventh was calm with fog . . . and so on.

But on the morning of the fifteenth there came a little air from the westward, and if the fog did not vanish quite immediately it became less wet; and the sails dried and were filled by that little air, and the ship began to move as I supposed (for I got no sights) in the right direction. And in the evening, as the breeze freshened, it became quite clear, though cloudy; and if I did not know exactly where I was I knew I was not going to hit anything. So I lost the last chance of using my deep-sea sounding machine, which I had carried carefully stowed away in its case all this voyage, for a little before midnight, as I expected, I saw the flash of the Fastnet Light in the sky. And that, says the reader, shows that I knew quite exactly enough where I was. Do not, dear reader, jump to conclusions. That is what I did. A very great authority, among his rules for cruising yachtsmen, puts, "Don't be careless about lights; time the flashes." I had not then read his book, but if I had, I should have laughed at the idea of mistaking the single flash of the Fastnet, repeated every five seconds, for anything else; I wrote in my log-book that I had seen the Fastnet, and laid off my position from the Fastnet on the chart, and steered along the coast. The coast somehow did not look quite right, but it was a dark night anyway.

At first dawn we were going along finely; right ahead

was a little black spike, obviously the Stag Rock off
Castle Haven. But as the light grew the coast became
very wrong indeed; it became in fact Brow Head instead
of Baltimore, and that rock 10 miles away was the Fastnet. No one had timed the flashes; what we had seen
last night was the fifteen-second light on the Bull Rock,
not the five-second light on the Fastnet as I had supposed.

I had the ship's number and her destination and her
last port ready bent on the signal halliards as we
approached the lighthouse, and was trying to manœuvre them so that they might not be hidden by the
nine sails I had set; and then I found all that was a waste
of labour, for the lighthouse burst into festoons of flags
with a congratulatory significance; and I had to haul
my hoists down in a hurry and express my thanks as
quickly as might be before my signal was indistin-
guishable in the distance; for we were actually sailing
this morning.

With a gentle westerly breeze, which indicated that
we had got on the right side of the anticyclone, behind
us, and three and a half days before us, for we were to
call at Wicklow on Friday night for final orders, there
seemed no reason why we should not go into Baltimore,
where my ship was built, and where K. was thinking of
placing an order for a copra-cutter, and as it turned out
we should have done very much better by staying there
until the Reception Committee gave us a tow the rest
of the way (as they would have had to do to avoid
spoiling their function). But the glass was still ominously high, and I carried on to the eastward; a little
freshening at night bringing us at daylight off the Saltee
Islands. All that day we looked at the Saltee Islands, but
in the evening we drifted past the Tuskar and from there

were again reported; two days to go and 50 miles to Wicklow.

That night the breeze came away fresh from the northward, and since my charts were very old and I knew the buoyage and the Wexford banks themselves had changed, I stood off shore and in again at dawn, and the wind left us off the Blackwater Lightship. What I cared about now was getting inshore, and into communication with a tug; we were 5 miles out, with no boat, and due in Wicklow, 30 miles away, next day. Before the tide turned against us we had got within 2 miles of the shore, and there anchored; but by then it was too dark for anyone to recognize us.

And when we weighed next morning I remembered that the coasters say they can make 9 miles up this coast on every tide; but I have not the local knowledge that the coasters have, and anyway, twice nine is eighteen, not thirty. Still if we could signal Wicklow Head all would not be lost; and an air of wind might come along. A little before the tide turned it did, and we were able to get within about 6 miles of the Head before we had to anchor again. But since, once the evening tide had made, nothing could do us any harm, the wind made belated amends and brought us in a very fine and showy manner right up to Wicklow Roads and there left us very calm and peaceful for the night; and we had earned some rest after all the pulley-hauling of ropes and heaving-up of anchors of the last two days. So my other sister came off to give me my Sailing Orders—she had been looking out for me from Wicklow Head most of the day—and the Customs Officer to give me pratique, for I knew I should get no formalities of that sort done next day, and it would be ridiculous to have the population of Dublin swarming on board with the yellow flag flying over all. As I began to suspect the kind of thing that was going to happen next day (no one foresaw it in the least, and the arrangements were quite inadequate for dealing with a crowd estimated at 30,000), I wished that I could lose myself somewhere between Wicklow and Dunleary, but it would not have been fair to the people who came out to see the show, nor to the Yacht Clubs who cancelled their programmes of races in order that all their boats might be available to escort me into the harbour.

I am not in the least sceptical about the capabilities of motor-launches or the reliability of their engines, but it would be a stiff job towing against the tide—and the ebb was running right up to the time fixed for my arrival—so I started with the first of the flood, at four in the morning, so as to try to get well up into Dublin Bay and drop back to the harbour on the ebb. But I could not; there was little wind till the tide turned, and then it came right ahead. I was driven back into Killiney Bay, and there for a fourth time I anchored. I did not anchor a fifth time, for I was towed up to Dunleary at the appointed time and on the firing of the third maroon—the first was preparatory when I was sighted; at the second, as I passed the pier-heads, every mast burst into bunting—I picked up the same moorings which I had let go exactly two years, to the second, previously.

But as for the cheering of crowds, the playing of bands, the making of speeches, the procession to Dublin headed by Neptune and Amphitrite in an allegorical car, these things have nothing to do with the voyage, but show an appreciation of it for which I am deeply thankful; it is good to have sailed round the world in order to be at home again.